On the Stoop

Macklyn W. Hubbell

Insight Press

New Orleans

Printed in the United States of America
ISBN 0-914520-30-X

To some people, things just happen. Others see the hand of God at work. I subscribe to the latter, for my adult life has been too satisfying to attribute it to fate. Two ladies have become a part of my adult life; and I dedicate this book to them: the mother, Ruth Gandy Melton, who gave birth to my wife and who has been a genuine source of inspiration to me, and to her daughter, my wife Bet, who "birthed" me into adult life with love, encouragement, and commitment.

Contents

Acknowledgements

Researching and writing *On the Stoop* has been pure pleasure. After completing my teaching assignments at New Orleans Baptist Theological Seminary and before beginning my professional counseling services at the Psychiatric Healthcare Center, I zipped in and around the New Orleans area to interview older residents whose lives and living are and have been as varied as flora in the marshes and fauna in the lakes, bayous, and Gulf. I never knew in advance of an interview what I would discover or how I would entitle it. By the time I finished, I was always amazed at the story I had heard and had the inspiration of a title.

To the dozens of persons I interviewed and to those whose stories lie within the covers of this book, I am grateful. I regret that I had to limit the number of personal interviews and resulting stories, but at some point I had to stop.

In addition to the special people interviewed and written about, I am indebted to Terri Walters for her word processing work, Kathleen Doran for her expert and meticulous editing, Bet Hubbell for accompanying me on many of the interviews and adding her special suggestions to the overall manuscript, and Polly Field Hubbell for her cover design.

On the Stoop

> Thus it is that I have now undertaken, in my eighty-third year, to tell my personal myth. I can only make direct statements, only 'tell stories.' Whether or not the stories are 'true' is not the problem. The only question is whether what I tell is my fable, my truth. (Carl Jung, *Memories, Dreams, Reflections*)

In the "ancient" days before the convenience of air conditioning and the luxury of television, some New Orleanians spent much of their time outside their singles, doubles, or whatever their dwelling type. Many of their hours outside were on the stoop. They sat chatting about the heat, the river, and personal happenings of the day. Hawkers passed with their wares, shouting their marketing jingles. One octogenarian mimicked what he remembered hearing from the walking sausage vendor: "I've got your liver, your blood, and your hot sausage." The words *hot sausage* were stressed and stretched, *H-O-T S-A-U-S-A-G-E.* Those peddling boiled crawfish hawked their mudbugs, and the ragman pushed his cart and invited stoop sitters and onlookers to bring to him their "rags, bottles, and bones."

Reflecting on her childhood, Leah Chase, a New Orleans restaurateur, remembered the "door poppers," the black children who peeped through the shutters during the early part of the day to view the goings-on in the street. It was only later in the afternoon or evening, when adults were present, that they were allowed in the street.

Like almost everything else, the stoops had to undergo cleaning by the residents. Oral history provides information relating to persons who remember that their stoops were scoured with pieces of brick. One New Orleanian added that knives and forks were cleaned in the same primitive fashion.

With the mental image of persons sitting around on their stoops, I decided to locate persons who were native-born or longtime residents of the Crescent City and who may not have been well publicized, but who have contributed to the overall uniqueness of the Big Easy. After discovering and meeting these wonderful people, I selected parts of their life stories for publication.

As you read these accounts of persons from here and there, in and around New Orleans, imagine a stoop setting with lively conversations. But remember that these people are reporting on personal events as they perceived them; no attempt at documenting their statements was made. They related their stories as they remembered them—the nature of oral history.

Momma's Colorblind

Living on the river side in a double house on Cadiz Street in uptown New Orleans is Lottie Mae Nickols Burnley, an attractive eighty-three-year-old with a friendly, magnetic personality who prefers to be called "Momma." She stands in her doorway and calls to new residents in her neighborhood to come over for her special blend of CDM and Community coffees. When her second husband Alfred, now deceased, was hospitalized and sharing a room with a young Pakistani man, Momma befriended the patient with goodies from her gourmet kitchen. When she displayed her crocheted and hand-sewn quilts at the New Orleans Jazz and Heritage Festival she met and warmly related to Rochelle Zolubis from New York, who wrote to her upon his return to the Big Apple:

> Dear Lottie Mae,
> I had a wonderful time visiting New Orleans for the Jazz Fest. One of the best parts of the trip was meeting you. Your kindness and warm smile made me so happy.

Those who love her and her cooking gather in her kitchen once a year for a feast of love and good food, which includes her stuffed peppers (with thirteen ingredients), mirlitons, fried chicken, crabs, and gumbo. Her four-burner Kitchen Queen gas stove gets a workout when everyone gathers at her house. As many as twenty-three of her children have crowded around the porcelain-top table in her narrow kitchen at one time. When Lottie Mae refers to her "children," she is not talking about her biological children, for she has never given birth. However, through her kindness she has given the gift of rebirth and renewed life to many people of diverse ethnic and racial backgrounds. When it comes to the color of someone's skin, Momma is colorblind. Color does not matter to her and her friends. She states that some people say, "I can't get along with so and so." "The reason is," she counsels, "You can't get along with yourself." Her relationship with God throughout the years has enabled her to maintain a "love thy neighbor as thyself" attitude.

Lottie Mae met one of her most special children in Canton, Mississippi, before she came to New Orleans. She was a young wife, married to Ike Davis, living on West Fulton Street, where they operated a grocery store. Across the street resided Ethel and Goldie Robinson, both blind, and their little son Stevie, also blind. The family was well below the federal government's poverty level guidelines. Stevie spent a lot of his playtime in and around the grocery store. The sales people were kind to him, giving him nickels, dimes, and quarters. Lottie Mae kept an empty fruit jar in the store for Stevie and encouraged him to put half of his gift money in the jar for safe-keeping—to be used for clothes and other necessities. Ethel Robinson knew about her son's fruit-jar money and one day came to borrow $3.37 to pay her electricity bill. J. D. Madness, a salesman who called on the Ike Davis Grocery, gave Lottie Mae $5.00 to buy Stevie some clothes; she bought him a pair of blue jeans, socks, two flannel shirts, a toothbrush, and toothpaste.

Stevie was taught not to beg from salesmen or customers in the Davis Grocery Store. Once Lottie Mae overheard Stevie enthusiastically exclaim about a customer's bag of lemon cookies—he was overwhelmed by the inviting lemon aroma. Lottie Mae sensed his dilemma, but gently admonished him as he sat outside the store, "Stevie, don't you beg."

The welfare visitors enrolled Stevie in the School for the Blind in Jackson, Mississippi. Lottie Mae packed his belongings in her car and took him to school, encouraging him, "Be a good boy and obey your teachers and one day you will be a great man." His parents later moved to St. Louis to work in a broom factory which employed sightless persons, but on a return trip to Canton, Ethel Robinson reported to Lottie Mae on Stevie's well-being: "I think Stevie is going to be a preacher," she stated proudly.

"Why?," asked Lottie Mae.

"Because he's always singing," responded Ethel.

He did not become a preacher. He became Stevie Wonder.

Lottie Mae first came to New Orleans in 1935, left shortly thereafter, and returned in 1960. Ike Davis passed away during that time. She then married Albert Burnley; she was widowed again in 1977. As a New Orleans resident, Momma has devoted her days to cooking for people, either in their homes or her own. Her record for the number of quarts of gumbo she prepared in one day is fifty-two. She even prepares her Thousand Island salad dressing from scratch.

When she is not cooking, she is quilting. When asked how many quilts she has handsewn or embroidered, she motioned her hand downward, "There's no telling." She pulled out quilt after quilt, identifying the patterns, "This one is called 'Road to California' or 'Drunkard's Path'. This one is named 'Robbing Peter to Pay Paul'. This one I named 'Sweet Lottie' and this one is 'Tulip'." To finish twelve squares on an embroidered quilt takes Lottie Mae 672 hours, working eight evenings for seven hours each night to complete one square. Her embroidered quilt has twelve squares.

Although Lottie Mae's life has not been colored by

the royal purple of prosperity, her attitude towards people has been consistently regal. When I walked through her shotgun double home, from the living room to the kitchen, I noticed framed pictures of her many friends hanging on the walls and sitting on her dresser, including autographed photographs taken with television's Hugh Downs when she was a guest on his "Over Easy" show in California. Her modest accommodations reflect a meager income of $427 a month, yet her refrigerator and freezer are full of foods prepared in her own kitchen. She originally invited me just to have a cup of her special-blend coffee. The invitation quickly expanded to include fried chicken, barbecued ribs, cabbage, and rice. Best of all, I was invited to be one of "Momma's children."

Bring Him Down

Emile and Cecile Labat founded their mortuary business in 1883 at North Rampart and Barracks Streets. The next generation, including Louis and Myrtle Labat Charbonnet, continued the service-oriented business. The Charbonnet-Labat Funeral Home is now located on the corner of St. Philip Street and Claiborne Avenue, beneath the shadow of Interstate 10 (I-10) and behind a row of banana trees.

Louis Charbonnet died in 1986, but eighty-six-year-old Myrtle and her four children (Phyllis Charbonnet Burns, Armand, Barbara Charbonnet Franklin, and Louis), with ages ranging from fifty-three upward, own and operate the funeral business and its expanded carriage and transportation subsidiaries. Their children, the next generation of Charbonnets, are also becoming involved in the family business. Louis, the youngest of the business partners, proudly boasts that, "You can't buy a better funeral from anybody else in New Orleans."

Among the diversified services offered by the old-line funeral home is the traditional jazz funeral, a part of the African-American subculture for decades. The Labats and the Charbonnets have been an important part of the ritual for decades also; in any given year, they will conduct as many as fifty jazz funerals. When a jazz musician or a second-liner dies, at the family's request, the Charbonnets will help "bring him down," that is, they will assist the mourners in providing a burial in grand, traditional style.

To the casual observer, a jazz funeral is simply one at which jazz music is played; however, the Charbonnets are sensitive to the differences in rituals and traditions. When a well-known jazz musician dies, strict protocol is followed. The mourning family invites fellow musicians to present a special musical tribute to the deceased. The official mourners and pallbearers wear tuxedos and the family dresses in mourning black. The primary service is conducted in a church, with briefer tributes paid before the funeral and at the cemetery.

A second-line funeral has some of the ritual of the jazz funeral, but with distinct differences. Second-lining means anybody or anything that is secondary to the primary activity. In this context, the primary activity is a funeral ritual conducted for a prominent musician; whereas, the secondary is a less elaborate ritual honoring the deceased—musician or not. The family simply requests a second-line funeral soliciting the help of friends and acquaintances.

More often than not, a second-line funeral will take place a week after the death. Since this funeral has added expenses, the mourners and friends need that much time to make arrangements for their personal costs, such as the rental of tuxedos and the extra funeral costs of hiring a jazz band; paying the City of New Orleans for two police motorcycle escorts (seventy-five dollars each); and providing food at a private club or "spot." To help the family defray the costs, the club will set up a cigar box or a similar container for patrons to contribute toward the costs.

One such club for the Treme Community is the Caldonia Bar, located on St. Philip Street one block (towards the river) from the funeral home. The Charbonnets recall that before Caldonia, Ruth's Cozy Corner on North Robertson Street and Ursulines Avenue was the focal point for collecting for second-liners' funeral expenses. Momma Ruth, as the proprietor was affectionately called, would customarily come to the Charbonnets and assume full responsibility for the funeral costs of a faithful patron and committed second-liner, ordering, "Give him a two-thousand-dollar funeral and I will collect the costs." Momma Ruth displayed the collection box on the counter at her club, encouraging generous contributions.

On the day of the second-line funeral, the casket is taken past the club—and maybe even brought into the club—for a final tribute with jazz music and dancing. This is traditionally referred to as "the pass"—passing by the favorite spot of the deceased. En route to the church from the Charbonnet-Labat Funeral Home, the traditional second-liners and the hired band lead the procession to the church. The second-liners will "cut the person loose" within a specified distance to allow the procession to proceed to the church. The second-liners, with their tambourines and cymbals, return to the club for celebration. Slow, dirgelike music is replaced with livelier, jazzed-up music as the mourners return to the club for drinks, food, and a general celebration. The official mourners and family members continue with church and burial services. When they "bring him down," they return to the home of the deceased for gumbo, fried chicken, and potato salad—just a sample of the foods awaiting the mourners. This ritual of returning to the home is referred to as the "re-pass."

Second-lining at a standard funeral is not uncommon, unexpected, or sacrilegious. For an example, when former Mayor Ernest ("Dutch") Morial died, thousands of second-liners joined in the procession as the official mourners left Gallier Hall and Saint Louis Cathedral. At times, second-lining may appear to be chaotic, but Louis Charbonnet maintains that, "No matter how unruly it appears, second-lining has structure. The solemnity is always there. Everybody knows that it is a funeral."

Hundreds of times a year, the Charbonnets are called upon for their professional services, just as Emile and Cecile Labat were in the last century. The third, and even fourth generations of the family continue to maintain their tradition of serving New Orleans residents with style and quality for standard, jazz, or second-line funerals.

Krasna of All Trades

Life for Krasna Briacich Karch in Sucora on the Yugoslavian island of Hvar from 1937 to 1955 was different from life for Krasna Vojkovich of New Orleans from 1955 forward. On this island in the Adriatic Sea, Krasna learned to do everything for her family and herself. It was a matter of survival.

During the first eight years of her life, World War II was either on its way to Yugoslavia or it had arrived. The Axis Forces from Italy occupied Krasna's home island, followed by a German takeover. When the Italians were on her island, she and her family spent time in the forest both day and night, seeking shelter from the horrors of war. When the Germans occupied Krasna's island, the civilians were transported by boats to the continent and by railroad boxcar to the Hungarian border. She and her youngest sister, along with her parents, huddled in a boxcar with livestock. Her mother spread herself like a mother hen over the girls to keep them from being trampled by the horses and cows in the boxcar.

While heading for concentration camps, the German guards became engaged in an unexpected battle, allowing Krasna and her family to escape. Eventually Krasna, with her sister Mlaolenka, returned to Hvar. Her two older sisters, who had been sent to Africa to stay with an aunt before the rest of the family was forced to leave the island, returned to Sucora dressed in black, thinking their family members were dead. Finally, her brother returned to the home island in 1946, after serving in the Yugoslavian Army and suffering from frostbite to his feet. Both the returning sisters and the liberated brother joyfully discovered that no one in their family had been killed.

During these days from 1937 to 1955, Krasna learned to do everything. She searched the beaches for rubber which had washed ashore to make shoes for herself and her family. Their home had been stripped of furniture, and the floors had been ripped up for use in German bunkers. Until scraps of the bunkers could be found, the family slept in the attic of their home. Seeds were shared by neighbors to plant greens, potatoes, turnips, and string beans. They picked figs and grapes and fished in the sea. Writing and spelling were practiced by scribbling in the topsoil. When a sheet of paper was available, she erased her writing in order for the sheet to be used over and over again. She learned to crochet, mend, and knit; she planted and harvested grain; and she made flour from the grain. Firewood was gathered to provide heat to bake the dough for their bread.

Krasna's journey to New Orleans began when John Vojkovich, who lived there, returned to his home island of Hvar to find a bride. He chose eighteen-year-old Krasna, the young lady who learned to do everything while living in Yugoslavia. She was Krasna of all trades.

Even though she left a life of hardship, Krasna loved her family and her home island. Oddly enough, coming to the security and affluence of the United States was frightening. The tall buildings and elevators in New York raised her anxiety level. When her new husband John brought her to New Orleans, she slowly relaxed when she viewed the Crescent City's tallest buildings, the Hibernia Bank Building and the Maison Blanche Building. These structures were small in comparison to New York's skyscrapers and not as frightening to her.

Krasna's forty-seven-year-old husband had come to New Orleans when he was fifteen. During John's thirty-two years in New Orleans, he worked first on an oyster boat with his father. It did not take him long to know that this kind of work was not for him. Next, he was introduced to the restaurant business at Kolb's Restaurant. By 1934, John was in a position to buy and operate his own restaurant on North Broad Street, the Crescent City Steak House. Because of his negative experiences harvesting oysters, he vowed that he would neither work in the Gulf of Mexico again nor serve seafood in his future restaurant. He kept his commitment; the Crescent City Steak House has served only beef—no seafood.

Having learned to do everything on the island, working long hours preparing and serving food was no problem for Krasna. The abundance of food awed her and the waste of food by customers pained her, but hard work never phased her. Even today, she mops the floor of the restaurant before the employees come to mop it again.

Krasna and John operated their restaurant on the ground level of their North Broad Street business and lived upstairs. They had four children (Frank, Marilyn, Zvenka, and Anthony) who learned to work in the restaurant, play behind the Crescent City Steak House, and sleep above it in their living quarters.

John died a couple of years ago, but Krasna and her son Anthony are maintaining the high standards of food preparation and service at the restaurant. The Vojkovich family feels that their customers want to return to the Crescent City Steak House to see the familiar. The booths for private dining and the tables and chairs are as they were decades ago. Printed menus were forced on them by law, but they still prefer for their customers to simply order a T-bone or a rib eye steak with a salad, without the bother of a printed menu.

Krasna continues to be impressed with local, state, and national politicians who eat regularly at her family's restaurant. Recently, a former customer called to see if the Crescent City Steak House was still open. He returned with his wife to sit in the booth where they sat while dating many years before.

Krasna, the lady of all trades, admits that restaurant work is hard, but she hopes her family will carry on in the Vojkovich tradition. Making bundles of money is not her goal. She and her family simply want to make a living while serving beef which is second to none in the Port City.

Fig Street Life

Olive, Fig, Apricot, and Apple are names reminiscent of the fragrances and tastes of an orchard. They are also the names of streets that intersect South Carrollton Avenue before it meets and defers to the grand St. Charles Avenue. Gertrude Alberta Crusta lived at 8800 Fig Street from the age of six until she married Otto Wille at age twenty-four. Fig Street is now lined with houses, but at that time it ran through cow pastures.

At her Fig Street home, Gertrude played jacks, batted a ball with a paddle, played on the swing in the backyard, and colored pictures. For special entertainment, she and her siblings packed a picnic basket and went to Palmer Park to hear musical ensembles play unrehearsed compositions. The Ashton Movie Theater was four or five blocks away across the pasture on Apple Street. The Saturday matinees only offered silent movies—Gertrude hadn't yet been introduced to the fancy "talking" movies. Walking home after the movie never posed a safety problem.

Gertrude's mother Christine got the neighborhood news each morning when she did the household shopping at the Cali Grocery and Meat Market on the corner of Fig and Eagle Streets. Once her mother heard that some members of a neighborhood family were "using needles." Gertrude wasn't sure what that meant, but she knew to walk on the other side of the street when she got near that house. Her father usually discounted her mother's market gossip, but Gertrude vows that it was "always accurate." Each afternoon at one o'clock her mother napped for an hour and a half. Coffee was served at three o'clock as a wake-up ritual.

Gertrude's Milan-born father was a conscientious family man. He transported his landscaping tools by wheelbarrow to and from jobs and made enough money for the Crustas to have chicken and potato salad on Sundays and beans and rice or macaroni with tomato gravy during the week. Whatever else was served at their meals came from their Fig Street garden: potatoes, string beans, cabbage, and spinach. A special Saturday treat was a plate full of waffles. On Sunday, as the budget permitted, she and her friends had ice cream topped with chocolate or strawberries during the season.

Her father was not Lutheran like her mother—he was Roman Catholic. On her parents' fortieth wedding anniversary, he lay gravely ill in the Baptist Hospital. He asked her mother what she wanted most from him. "I want us to have communion together." They did. He died the next day.

Childhood diseases like mumps, measles, and whooping cough made the rounds among the Crusta children. When they were sick with a communicable disease, the Board of Health put a Quarantine sign—black background with red letters—on their door. The sign stayed up and visitors stayed away until the threatening sign could be removed. If the Crusta children had the sniffles or a cold, a dose of citrate magnesium was generously given and reluctantly taken.

Tragedy struck her family when her seventeen-year-old-brother died. Her mother wore black and she and her sisters wore black-and-white mourning clothes for a year. Her mother insisted that they wear mourning garments to show respect for her brother's memory.

Gertrude's church was a meaningful part of her life. The dominant emotion she felt about the Bible and her Immanuel Lutheran Church (now Grace Lutheran) was awe. Her pastor, the Reverend O. J. Schilling, meant business. He was honored and respected, and like God, was to be feared. Gertrude and her five siblings never thought about misbehaving—they didn't dare—not with the Reverend Schilling, their mother, and God around. No matter how she was feeling, she always took her Saturday-night bath, got up early the next morning, put on her homemade Sunday dress (she had only two other dresses for weekdays), and boarded the streetcar for church. (If she missed church, it meant she must be sick, and that always meant a dose of castor oil.) When she reached age twelve, she began attending confirmation classes after school three afternoons a week for a year. She learned everything from the Apostles' Creed to the books of the Bible. At nighttime, whenever Gertrude and her brothers and sisters came in, they approached their parents' bed for their good-nights and prayers, "Now I lay me down to sleep. . . . God bless mother, daddy, aunts, uncles. . . ."

The Christmas celebrations at the Immanuel Lutheran Church were special. The tree, which reached from the floor to the ceiling, was decorated and also strung with popcorn. The artificial grapes on the tree inspired Reverend Schilling to elaborate on holy communion. After the holy service on Christmas Eve, Gertrude and her church friends recited poems and played musical instruments. Then came the big event: Christmas candy, nuts, apples, and oranges for the children.

Birthdays at the Crusta home were celebrated with the traditional yellow cake decorated with candles for the "birth child." The children requested and received their favorite dishes, provided they were available. On her sixteenth birthday, Gertrude got the gift of gifts, a Singer sewing machine. This was the beginning of her career as a professional seamstress, which she pursued as an adult. That same year she met Otto Wille outside the Waldo Burton Memorial Home for Boys on South Carrollton Avenue.

They wanted their courtship to begin right away, but before Otto was allowed to talk to Gertrude, her father wanted to hear Otto's life story. For their dates they either took a streetcar ride to the Orpheum Theater for a movie or went on an outing to Palmer Park. As a child, Gertrude loved the Mardi Gras parades, especially the *flambeaux* (flaming torches carried to illuminate the parade), and she and Otto continued to enjoy them together. They viewed the parades on St. Charles Avenue, standing near Beakman's Men Store and the Arcade to have shelter from rain or cold. The only parade "throws" then were beads; later, the krewe members threw tops and buttons from the floats.

The romantic juices continued to flow, and Gertrude and Otto decided to marry, so Otto formally requested the consent of Gertrude's father. It was granted, although Otto was unemployed at the time and had made only thirty-seven cents an hour at the peak of his employment. Subsequently, he proved that he could provide for Gertrude and their daughter Joan.

Gertrude Crusta Wille, now age eighty-one, no longer lives on Fig Street, but her memorable Fig Street experiences live on in her.

A Foursome for Life

Identical twins Laurette and Juliette Hecker did everything alike—they dressed alike, ate the same foods, drove the same car, and even had toothaches at the same time. Cornelius, one of their older brothers, referred to them simply as "the Twins." Thus, it was understandable that when they married, they chose men who were close friends. Eric Dahlstrom was an electrician trained at Isaac Delgado Central Trades School (now Delgado Community College) and Louis Cook was a printer receiving his training at the same institution.

They were married—Laurette to Eric and Juliette to Louis—in a double wedding ceremony on October 22, 1931, at their home at 4007 St. Charles Avenue. At the invitation of the girls' mother, Julia Riggers Hecker, the two couples moved into the spacious Hecker home, joining two other sisters and their husbands, a brother and his wife, and an unmarried brother. The Victorian house had twenty-seven rooms and nine and a half bathrooms, allowing the extended family sufficient room for both company and privacy. Mother Julia never asked for any payment of room or board. The families continued to live there for seventeen years after the twins' wedding, separating and moving away only after Julia's death.

Twinship continued for Laurette and Juliette after marriage. Their first children (boys) were born within months of each other, but the second birth for each (boys again) was spaced farther apart—fifty months.

Everything, including jewelry, was the same. If one sister had something, the other had it too. Louis, with Eric's consent, usually did the shopping for special occasions such as Christmas. He didn't buy just one dress, he bought two. The girls alternated making decisions about what they would wear—Laurette chose one week and Juliette the next. If there was a slip up—one was wearing something, e.g., earrings, that the other wasn't—the error was immediately corrected. Louis and Eric, of course, did not dress alike. Colored threads sewn into their clothing identified ownership.

When Julia Hecker died, Laurette and Eric and Juliette and Louis and the four boys moved to their new residence, a high-low at 240 Bonnabel Boulevard in Metairie. The Bonnabel residence had only seven and a half rooms, much smaller than their former home. The four boys' bedrooms were upstairs and the two couples' rooms were downstairs. The meal menus were chosen alternately by the ladies while the men shared the traditional male chores, such as house repairs, yard work, and trash removal. When vacation time came, the families traveled together to places like the Smoky Mountains and the Caribbean. They bowled, played golf, and went to Mardi Gras parades—together.

Believe it or not, the Cooks and the Dahlstroms did some things separately. They kept separate bank accounts, although they divided expenses evenly. They also had different religious affiliations: Baptist, Evangelical, and Christian Scientist. Even the twins acknowledged that there was one difference between them, their dexterity at softball. Laurette was the better hitter, so she batted for Juliette without either the home or visiting coaches ever realizing the switch.

The Dahlstroms and Cooks delight in recalling stories. Before the family moved to St. Charles Avenue, the young Hecker twins were reared at 7632 Hampson Street (the house is still owned by Laurette and Juliette). It is a source of family pride that the house is the one in which author John Kennedy Toole lived and wrote his Pulitzer Prize winning novel, *A Confederacy of Dunces*.

Louis smiles when he recalls their first Christmas on Bonnabel Boulevard. A fire in the garage consumed their hidden Christmas stockings. As the firemen were leaving after extinguishing the blaze, Louis expressed his gratitude to them with the gift of a bottle of whiskey which had been given to them by their friend Peter Jacobs. It was after the firemen left that they realized that Peter had tricked them. He had replaced the whiskey with tea. After becoming aware of the error, Louis and Eric promptly went to the fire station and replaced the tea with the "real thing."

Not all their stories are happy ones. On August 5, 1982, Juliette underwent routine knee surgery. Although the corrective surgery was successful, she lapsed into a comatose state—possibly a reaction to one or more medications—from which she has never recovered. Six years later, Eric suffered a fall which has left him incapacitated.

The Dahlstrom and Cook children did not continue the tradition of living together. Richard and Louis Cook, Jr., and John and Robert Dahlstrom moved out and away. After fifty-nine years, however, the original four still live together, although Juliette is confined to a hospital bed and Eric to a chair. Today there is a loving concentration on the wounded mates. It was obvious that Louis spoke for both couples when he smiled broadly and said, "We would do it all over again."

City Mouse

Early happenings have a way of getting lost in the memory maze or becoming irretrievable—except those memories that stand out as especially happy or sad. Louise Johnson Franklin, born between the Spanish American War and the war to end all wars (World War I), remembers an event which happened when she was five or six years old. Her Aunt Leona made her a black taffeta coat, which she wore proudly to kindergarten. Since she was wearing such a pretty coat, her teacher selected Louise to be in a school play being cast that day. Her teacher gave her a choice of portraying either a country mouse or a city mouse. She chose to be the city mouse.

Louise, the city mouse, was born uptown on Eighth Street, but she did most of her growing up at 2201 Gordon Street, east of the Industrial Canal. In an intervening period, she lived with her Aunt Caroline, called Nanan, on St. Andrew Street. If the city mouse misbehaved in any way, Nanan threatened to put her in the attic where the devil was. In her young imagination, the sun shining through the cracks leading to the attic looked like fire. Young Louise never wanted to be confined to the attic where the fire burned and the devil lived—she behaved herself at Nanan's house.

The decision to move to 2201 Gordon Street was made by her father, a Baptist minister who also owned and operated a grocery store. He decided to move after her brother Benny was injured when he fell, as children are prone to do, on the newly paved South Broad Street. The Reverend Johnson did not want his children exposed to the dangers of a paved street, so he moved his family to a safer location.

On Gordon Street, the city mouse had plenty of safe room to roam. She got cockleburs in her hair and caught her neighbor's cows by the tails to deter them from getting into the garden. She bought a bucket of clabber for ten cents from her neighbor Mrs. Branch. She went to the McCarty school, but she had to hurry home after school to work. She tended to her siblings and cooked for her mother. She bought bread from the LaNasa Bakery and delivered the loaves to her father's customers before she went to school. Play came only after work. Only when her mother had company was she free to play.

Louise has added a number of decades to her life since she received the honor of being the city mouse. In her résumé, written a decade ago, she wrote:

My interest and emphasis has always been in helping people to help themselves. I'm presently seeking the opportunity to use the additional skills acquired in my various job assignments.

I'm open to any situation that will afford me the chance to continue to make a meaningful impact on the lives of others as well as utilize my skills in housing, arts, crafts, filing, and cosmetology.

Louise Franklin wrote her résumé when she was well into her eighth decade of life. By that time, she had already been graduated from Poro Beauty College and Rabouin Evening School, where she majored in sewing. By the time she entered her ninth decade, she had graduated as a nursing assistant. She has chosen not to pursue a nursing career, but she has maintained her practice of pressing and shampooing hair. Customers call for appointments and show up for her services offered in the front room of her blond brick home on Feliciana Street. Louise learned to work early in her life and continues to do so even now. In fact, her eagerness to learn is so high that she refuses to associate with anyone who "doesn't know anything."

Work for Louise does not have to be for remuneration. She is a volunteer for Saint Philip's Apostles' Senior Citizen Center where she teaches arts and crafts. Her sewing experience allows her to sew for the NORD Golden Age Club, making evening gowns for their annual ball at the Lions Center on Tchoupitoulas Street. She makes the vestments for the priests at Saint Mary of the Angels Catholic Church. She smiles as she complains about her pastor being too active in his vestments—wearing them out too soon.

The city mouse has been and continues to be busy in life. Her services have not gone unnoticed. President Jimmy Carter and Mayors Ernest Morial and Sidney Barthelemy have recognized Louise's volunteer contributions.

Driving and guiding Louise Johnson Franklin have been these directives from her parents:

Work and pray.

Be honest.

Go to Sunday School and read the Bible.

Share yourself with others.

She still commits to work and prayer daily. She is honest. She considers Sunday School to be an integral part of her life. She has reared at least twenty children born to others and extended herself to scores of people here and there throughout Orleans Parish and beyond.

Badge No. 50

Pinned to his blue uniform shirt is his badge, with a star in the center, an inverted quarter moon above it symbolizing the Crescent City, and the number *50* engraved on it. It seemed appropriate in this case that the badge was located in the general area of the officer's heart. Captain John Harrison Hughes, Jr., field supervisor for the New Orleans Police Department, strongly believes that a certain genetic makeup is necessary for a person to be a law officer. As he puts it, "Police officers are born, not made."

In the case of John and his brother George, however, there was certainly no obvious family background to indicate that the two sons of John Harrison Hughes, Sr., and Mildred Cahalan Hughes might become police officers. Harrison, as their father was called, was a banker; his mother came from the Klotz family, of the Klotz Cracker Factory on Tchoupitoulas Street. George Hughes joined the New Orleans Police Department first, followed three years later by John in 1959. George resigned to become Chief of Police in Ohio, but John has remained with the NOPD.

Captain Hughes has observed the inevitable changes which occur in any profession. While administrative and policy changes are not always immediately evident to the general public, changes in the force's uniform and equipment are. Shortly before John joined the NOPD, officers' uniform shirts were gray; they were changed to long-sleeved blue shirts with ties, followed by short-sleeved blue shirts and no ties. The black-and-white patrol cars were replaced with blue-and-white cars, and the red flashing lights on the cars were replaced with blue lights so they could be more easily distinguished from other emergency vehicles. Patrol cars were eventually staffed with one patrolman instead of two, and battery-operated (walkie-talkie) radios became standard equipment, allowing communications with officers at all times.

According to Captain Hughes, criminal types have remained consistent from one decade to the next, except for the increased use of mind-altering drugs. He noted that a high percentage of police officers are still injured when responding to domestic cases. Computerized dispatch systems have remarkably reduced the police response time, although calls for police assistance have risen from about thirteen thousand per month in the 1960s to forty thousand per month in the 1990s.

Captain Hughes is aware of the risks of his profession, but nevertheless he has been a committed officer for over thirty years. Having chosen not to marry, he has been able to be available in special ways. For instance, in 1970 he was returning from duty on Mardi Gras day when he noticed that the door to his neighborhood fire station was open and that the station was unattended. He stopped to close the door and decided to take a few extra minutes to prepare a fresh pot of coffee for the firemen when they returned. He was startled by an intruder. Officer Hughes "threw down on him." With the intruder's hands up, Hughes ordered him to lie down to be searched. With the barrel of his gun up against the intruder's head, Hughes feigned trigger-finger nervousness. The intruder got the message; he volunteered that he had a loaded .32 caliber revolver in his right-hand pocket. Officer Hughes disarmed him, then took backward steps to a nearby telephone to call for a backup. Earlier that Mardi Gras day, one officer had been shot and killed and another had been wounded. The man in Officer Hughes's custody was not involved in that crime, but at that point in time he had no way of knowing and was taking no chances.

When Captain Hughes goes on duty at ten o'clock each evening, he is in charge of the NOPD for the night. The Loyola University graduate maintains that he and his officers must have a close relationship with the community. Persons may call in to have an officer investigate a leak in the plumbing or to allay fears about a rattling set of window blinds. He treats his fellow officers like family, praising them when they are good and scolding them when necessary. He takes care of them, and they work for and with him. In response to a question about Captain Hughes, a fellow officer said, "We all like to work for him."

The Captain's glass of iced coffee was empty, and my hot tea had cooled. Our conversation was winding down. It was ten o'clock and time for the Captain to call in and report, "I'm 108 now," meaning, "I'm on duty." Ironically, I later learned that as we sat and chatted a few extra minutes, an armed robbery was taking place just a short distance from my home. It was a very secure feeling knowing that there are men like Captain Hughes out there to "protect and serve."

From Chicken to Shrimps

On the corner of St. Claude and St. Roch Avenues is Lama's St. Roch Market, a gray rectangular building, forty feet wide, and four times that in length. On the St. Claude Avenue side of the building are rows of A-frame signs which read:

HOT WELL-SEASONED BOILED
TURKEY NECKS, PIG FEET, CHICKEN LEGS
WELL-SEASONED BOILED
SHRIMPS
FRESHLY BOILED DAILY

_____

TRY OUR B.B.Q.
CHICKEN AND RIBS
BEST JAMBALAYA
IN TOWN

_____

A sign attached to the building reads:

YOUR WIFE CALLED AND SAID
TO BRING HOME SOME
BOILED CRAWFISH AND PO-BOYS.

_____

The St. Roch Market was much different in 1949 when Anthony and Gloria Lama first opened their stall to sell chickens on foot for fifty to seventy-five cents apiece. The chickens were supplied by Anthony's brother, who made frequent trips to Texas to purchase chickens for customers in New Orleans. The Lama stall was just one among many at the St. Roch Market in the late 1940s and early 1950s. Other merchants in their designated spaces sold fruits, vegetables, and seafood.

Inevitably, change was on its way. Supermarkets came into existence and began to sell dressed chickens cheaper than Anthony could sell them in his stall. The other merchants in the market chose to fold up. Eventually the Lamas were left in the market alone with their new line of products: shrimp, crabs, oysters, crawfish, and other meats of the Gulf.

Upon entering the old New Orleans Market, to the right is an area for preparing and serving po-boys and hot meals. Beyond the sandwich and plate-lunch area are refrigerated display cases, stretching across the width of the building, where fresh seafood and boiled crawfish, shrimp, crabs, potatoes, and corn are sold. Although most customers get take-out orders, those who choose to eat their meal in the market may sit at one of the dozen or so small tables, with two chairs at each. The wooden captain's chairs provide more comfort than do the upright metal chairs, upholstered in red or brown vinyl. Natives from South Louisiana can easily be spotted by the way they eat crawfish—head-sucking and tail-squeezing, which are characteristic of veteran mudbug eaters. Dining is informal; a canned soft drink is available for fifty cents from either of the two vending machines.

Behind the refrigerated display units are the storage and preparation areas, where the large quantities of seafood are made ready for customers, including the restaurant owners who buy bulk quantities for their retail businesses. In the rear of the market is the office area, enclosed from the food service area, where the Lamas conduct the market's business affairs.   Until recently, Anthony and Gloria Lama owned and operated the market and were assisted by their son Tony.   They've now changed places; ownership and management have been transferred to Tony, and Anthony and Gloria continue to help in the market.

Work at the market for the Lamas was taxing, starting at six o'clock in the morning and lasting for ten to twelve hours a day, six days a week.   Offspring Gloria, Ann Marie, and Tony contributed their parts growing-up. On Saturday nights the Lamas treated themselves to ice-cream cones.   The Lamas say that the hard work at the market enabled them to provide their children with "nice clothes and good schools."

Anthony's philosophy for working and living was simple:

Work to survive.

Pay cash.

Be decent and straight.

Live by the Golden Rule.

A strong religious faith was modeled for Anthony by his mother.   When his brother Joe's appendix ruptured, Anthony's mother vowed to God, "Save him and I'll go to Mass every day." God did his part and so did Mrs. Lama.   She got up every morning at three o'clock to get ready for Mass, maintaining a perfect record for sixty years.

Characteristic of his life, Anthony's religious faith and outlook is simple.   Following the example of his mother, he and Gloria go to Mass at Saint Maria Goretti Catholic Church every Sunday.   After suffering a heart attack a few years ago, he says his goal for life now is "to breathe." He is doing well, and has had enough breath to go to Italy and Las Vegas. As for the rest of his life, Anthony, the "Merchant of Chickens and Shrimps," says it is left up to the "Man upstairs."

Whatcha Want, Sweetie?

At the apex of the triangle formed by Old Gentilly Road and Chef Menteur Highway is Richard's Restaurant. True to its advertisement, it remains open twenty-four hours a day and serves Northern coffee, breakfast, and fried chicken. Richard's has more variety on its menu than the listing on the faded Coca-Cola sign above the window on the side of the restaurant would suggest.

There is a steady stream of customers: workers in their hard hats, police officers in their uniforms, and an assortment of casually dressed people seated at one of the four booths, five tables, or the ten stools aligned with the stainless steel counter. Serving these hungry patrons are seven waitresses who work at various times during a twenty-four-hour period. Among them is petite Dorothy Lee Waldrop—she is under five feet tall—walking among the customers, her head tilted to one side, asking Richard's customers, "Whatcha want, Sweetie?" This sixty-four-year-old waitress worked for a brief time as an apprentice waitress at the Union Station and the Broadview Restaurant, but she is now a yeoman waitress, having worked at Richard's for nearly four decades.

Neither Dorothy nor the other six waitresses wear traditional waitress garb; they simply wear trousers and a smock with large pockets. As she slowly walks from table to table taking orders from her customers, she reassures

those awaiting service, "Get you in a minute, Sweetie."
She also offers advice to the hungry diners. I wanted a
half-order of pancakes, but she insisted that I get the full
order, "It all costs the same." When asked about the fried
chicken, she insists that it's the best in town. Maybe she
is biased, for this happens to be her favorite dish.

She loves her work and it shows, "I love to wait
on people. They are nice." When asked about tips, she
registered disappointment, "They're not too good. No-
body is working. These are hard times." What is a good
tip day? For Dorothy, making five dollars on tips is a
good day. The signs above the service area behind the
counter reflect what Dorothy says about the times:

ALL TICKETS WILL BE
PAID IN ADVANCE
BETWEEN THE HOURS OF
10:00 P.M. and 7:00 A.M.

PLEASE, IF YOU DON'T
BUY IT HERE, DON'T
EAT OR DRINK IT HERE.
THANK YOU.

Dorothy's life has been simple since her early
years in rural Alabama. She terminated her formal education after the ninth grade. Although she had to walk two
miles to school, this was not the reason she quit—she
needed the work. At age sixteen she was hired by the
cotton mill. Her Baptist upbringing included a county
church with dinner on the grounds and singing all
around. Her mother's directives are etched in her memory: "Don't put more on your plate than you can eat." and
"Treat people the way you would like to be treated."

Dorothy has been a resident of New Orleans for
nearly forty years. Her pronunciations and inflections
suggest that she is a Ninth Ward New Orleanian.

Returning to Alabama is not an option with Dorothy. She likes living in the Crescent City and expects to remain here working as long as she can.

Dorothy would like to travel. Once she went to New York City to visit a friend, but all she remembers is the height of the buildings. Someday she would like to go to Las Vegas and gamble. She doubts that she will make it, so she would be satisfied to stay in New Orleans and "win the lottery."

In the meantime, she will keep on working at Richard's, spending her spare time shopping at a mall, having her hair done on Thursdays, and pleasantly asking her customers, "Whatcha want, Sweetie?"

Beyond Centenarian

On February 20, 1993, Dagmar Renshaw LeBreton will have reached two years beyond centenarian status. Compared to millions in the United States, she will be among the honored thousands.

In her formative years from 1891 forward, Dagmar (one of thirteen children, eight girls and five boys) lived in a three-storied house at 935 Barracks Street. The French Quarter house, formerly owned by her family, is still standing. Today it is painted pink and trimmed in white with faded green shutters. A second-story balcony extends over the sidewalk, above one door and two shuttered windows. The second floor is symmetrical with the first, but the third floor has three recessed rectangular windows. From the top floor Dagmar watched and listened to the blacks who lived across the way, frying and eating catfish. Reflecting on the music she heard, her unresearched comment was, "I guess I heard jazz music in its beginning stages."

Henry and Maria Renshaw lived in the house with their thirteen offspring, their mothers, and two unmarried sisters. Henry, one of the first to be graduated from Tulane University Law School, had a love for knowledge blended with missionary zeal to share his accumulated facts with his thirteen children. Dagmar added, "I was educated at home by my father who lived and breathed the Bible and Shakespeare." This father-inspired home education was just a foundation. In addition to the great literature taught in their home were instructions from a Biblical school on Tonti Street; lessons were taught in French in the mornings and in English in the afternoons. Dagmar crowned her education with a certificate in art from H. Sophie Newcomb College, later receiving a bachelor of arts degree in languages from the same uptown institution.

With a mind as clear as most middle adults, Dagmar, referred to as *Tante* (French for "aunt") by many of her family members, had a walker nearby—the only visible sign of her disability from a broken hip six years ago—as we chatted about her life and philosophy. She wore a green cotton dress and white stockings with embossed designs. A bar pin was attached to the top of her dress and a Canterbury Cross on a black cord rested beneath the pin. She wore thick eyeglasses because of the cataract surgery she had undergone years ago. I tried to imagine what she looked like when she married Edmond LeBreton at age twenty-one. She smiled as she said that she was an ugly girl. She grew to be five feet and five inches, with light brown hair "as straight as nails." Her contradictory claim to beauty was that she was the ugliest child her mother had. When she wore a bonnet, her hair stuck up through it. Even her grandparents shook their heads at her features. Whatever she looked like as a girl on Barracks Street, she has developed into a *grande dame,* sitting and reflecting like the great lady she is.

She and Edmond married in 1912, but he died of pneumonia a year later, leaving her alone with a baby boy named for him. Teaching was her professional love, to which she committed herself in public and private schools before joining the faculty at Newcomb College where she taught both French and Italian. Even as she converses now, she uses French words almost as frequently as English. French words seem to express her thoughts better.

Not rambling, but with purposeful intention, Dagmar recalled her childhood days on Barracks Street.

Intergenerational living had its pluses, but at times she felt that too many adult eyes were focused on her. One of her two live-in grandmothers, Solidelle LeGardeur, whose room was near the stairway on Barracks Street, would chide her for child-noises, "Don't go up shouting like Choctaw Indians!" Or she would offer her a penny to keep quiet.

Serving flaming plum pudding at Christmastime was a family tradition she insisted on perpetuating. Even the sprig of holly on top of the pudding became a necessary part of this annual experience, which she discontinued only after she broke her hip.

Her paternal grandmother, Eliza Rebecca White Renshaw, bequeathed to her a love for plants. Behind the three-story dwelling on Barracks was a cistern to collect water for general household use as well as water for the periwinkles on top of the tank and the banana tree nearby. In her backyard, Dagmar watched Grandma Renshaw tend to her plants while she lifted the bricks to observe insects scurry for shelter. Background music for this idyllic scene was provided by the Renshaws' caged canary.

For the last twenty-five years she has lived at 1561 Calhoun Street, a block off St. Charles Avenue, where she has continued her love for New Orleans flora. By her own admission, her garden with its azaleas, roses, and irises—blessed by a Francis of Assisi bird feeder—is not what it was when she and her sisters Yvonne, Yolande, Margo, and Gladys first moved to her uptown double shotgun residency. (By the way, they all lived together as siblings even when their ages ranged from ninety to one hundred.) She is not able to keep up her garden now as she did when she was less than one hundred years old.

Life at nearly a hundred is "wonderful" with all its surrounding "mysteries." To be sure, arthritic pain and lazy eyes distract her focus, but only momentarily. Life continues to be wonderful for Tante as she accumulates knowledge and adds on wisdom, "Life is not a nuisance."

If she could go around life again, she would like to be a Will Rogers and make people laugh.

Doing Hair

Mary Louise Smith Rouser and Beonville Idelbert Rouser both "do hair." Beonville moved from Jackson, Mississippi, in 1949 and did hair on Rampart Street; Mary Louise joined her husband a year later, but she also worked on the riverfront with T. Smith Company, sweeping up coffee and sewing coffee bags, until 1953 when she had the clientele to return to doing hair full time.

When Mary Louise resumed working at her profession, she charged her patrons fifty cents each. The technique she used was referred to as "pressing hair." The fifty-cent treatment included straightening the client's hair with a comb heated on the stove (she used a pressing iron on very curly hair) and adding curls using a special curling iron. Clients who wanted a wave received the "Marcel" treatment. Prices for her beauty services increased to eight dollars for a wash and set, while a permanent wave was twenty dollars.

Mary Louise Rouser did more than hair; she gave advice to her clients. To teenagers she counseled:

Go to church.

Change your ways.

Get a job.

Don't steal.

On the Stoop

Don't destroy property.

Christmas and Easter seasons are to hairdressers what April 15 is to accountants. Before Christmas day, New Year's Eve, and Easter Sunday, clients lined up outside of Bernadette's Beauty Box on Danneel Street, where Mary Louise worked, to get their hair done. They formed queue early in the morning, long before the shop opened at eight o'clock. On any given Christmas and Easter, Mary Louise didn't finish doing hair until either the wee hours of the next morning or after the sun rose. Mary Louise remembers that one of her inebriated customers chose a hairstyle that she (the customer) vigorously objected to when she sobered up a few days later.

In 1984 Beonville Idelbert moved from South Rampart and Dryades Streets, where he did hair, to his own Ideal Barber Shop on the ground floor of their Pine Street residence. Unfortunately, Mary Louise's illness terminated her hairdressing career in 1989, but Beonville continues his work as a barber. The Ideal Barber Shop is furnished with typical equipment: three barber chairs, a shampoo bowl, a sterilizer cabinet for tools, and eight variously shaped mirrors. When asked about the mirrors, Beonville responded, "I use those to cut hair." When he was in barber school, his instructors taught him to look in the mirror to cut hair. One client, unfamiliar with his cutting style, chided him for looking in the mirror at himself, "I'm not paying for you to look at yourself." Beonville took time to explain that haircuts look different in the mirror than they do to the barber observing only inches away from the client's head.

Beonville was able to earn enough money to maintain a decent living for his family, even though haircuts ranged from only thirty-five to fifty cents. Barbering has changed, however. According to Beonville, cuts change every twelve to fifteen years—the hairstyle cycle. He says clients used to ask for flattops and now they want "funny styles and parts all over their heads."

"People do not respect their barbers anymore," Beonville pensively reflected, adding with a note of regret, "They do it themselves or have someone else to cut their hair."

Because of his age and health, Beonville's Ideal Barber Shop is not open to walk-ins. He has about twenty-five regular clients, like Messrs. Young, Washington, Matthews, Wilson, and Miller. As Beonville and I chatted, a client named Edward Jones was getting his standard "brush cut." Mr. Jones interrupted our conversation, emotionally and with nostalgia, "He's a good barber. He's been cutting my hair for twenty-five years. I waited a week for him this time." Beonville heard the compliment, but did not respond. He kept right on cutting Mr. Jones's hair with his fifteen-inch, German-made scissors.

As we ended our conversation, I noticed a blue travel bag containing clippers, scissors, and blades. Beonville responded to my inquiry about it, "I take my tools upstairs every night. I don't want anybody to use my tools." He implied that he did not even want his son and daughter, who are part-time "doers of hair," to use his tools.

Doing hair is not all the Rousers have done. Mary Louise and "Brother," as she calls Beonville, have reared eleven children—Leandra, Mary Ann, Beonville, Kenneth, Wendlyn, Gwendlyn, Larry, Romero, Leticia, Keith, and Mica. With a sigh of relief, Mary Louise proudly stated that none of her children has ever been in handcuffs or gotten killed in the city. All of their children are successfully employed (except Mica, who is retarded). Two of their children are ministers: Keith in the Baptist Church and Leticia in the United Church of Christ. How did they do hair and rear eleven children? Their rules were simple:

Listen to your parents.

Don't stand outside on the street or street corners.

On the Stoop

Boys have to be in by 9:00 P.M.

Girls have to be in at dark.

Misbehaving neighborhood children are sent home.

Do not go to parties without parents' knowledge of the environment at the parties.

Do not talk back to parents.

Every Sunday is church day. Afternoon play is allowed between morning church and night church.

Have fun in the house with television, books, and games.

Number, Please?

Mary and Albert Geiseler opposed the idea of any of their daughters working. They wanted Mary, Dora, and Jenni to stay in their home at Calliope and Clio Streets. Dora, however, was not to be dissuaded from working. In 1919, at age twenty-four, she applied for a job as a telephone operator at Southern Bell Telephone and Telegraph Company (now South Central Bell). She went to work the very next day and would work there for the next forty-one years without missing a day. If she was not asking, "Number, please?" she was directing the repairmen to locations needing service.

Dora commuted to work on the streetcar, boarding at Nashville Avenue and Magazine Street, then transferring at Canal Street. She always arrived for work on time at the Telephone Company building on Poydras Street. She says she "had a knack for handling the public, even though I could not see them." When the calls came through, she responded, "Number, please?" and proceeded to plug the caller's line into the board. When callers requested the telephone numbers for hotels or other public places, she knew them instantly. She became a human directory as her mind memorized the numbers repeatedly requested.

Life for Dora before her "Number, please?" days was one happy time after another. Her parents, Albert Fred and Mary Heuer Geiseler, were a bit possessive of their offspring Mary, Charlie, Joseph, Dora, Willie, Albert,

Johnny, and Jenni, but happiness far outshone their pos-
sessiveness. "We had wonderful times and had a
wonderful family," reflected Dora, now ninety-seven years
old.

The entire Geiseler family shared an enthusiasm
for Mardi Gras parades. Dora remembers that as a little
girl she went to a location near her home where Mardi
Gras floats were built. The workers lifted her onto the
floats where the kings and queens sat. Dora became
queen, if only for a few fleeting moments. Her father
built a donkey cart to carry his children to view the parades on the corner of Calliope Street and St. Charles
Avenue. Only her brother Joe refused to ride in the don-
key-drawn cart, "You expect me to ride with all that
crowd [his seven siblings]?" Her father, an engineer employed by Berwick Lumber Company, also built a
train—complete with engine, coaches, and tracks—for his
children to ride on in the backyard.

By her own admission, Dora was a tomboy; she
didn't like typical "girl-things." She would rather climb a
utility pole, which she did, and about which her mother
said, "Girls don't do those things." Playing baseball
ranked high on her recreational list; she was the pitcher
for the girl's baseball team at McDonogh No. 14 on Napoleon Avenue. She also remembers playing jacks and be-
longing to a sewing circle.

The sewing circle was composed of her uptown
girlfriends. Had it been strictly a domestic sorority focused on cutting and stitching, Dora would never have
been a part of it, for even her mother considered her a
failure as a seamstress. Her mother once cut out six
pattern pieces for "balloon-like drawers" and instructed
Dora to sew them together. Dora confesses that she got
the cutout parts all mixed up and that her mother gave
up on her as a seamstress. Dora's interest in the sewing
circle lay in the social dimension of the group. Each
member of the sewing circle contributed ten dollars a
month to hire a band for dances, which they had

regularly.

Since their dances were held in private homes (her father disallowed rented halls), like a Cinderella scene, the band could play only until midnight, because playing past that hour would have been too disturbing for the neighbors. After the music stopped, her sister's lemon pie was served with New Orleans' blended coffee.

Dora knew how to manipulate her stern father, however. Even though he said, "No," to dances in halls, he gave in one time when Mildred Walsdorf (whose father owned the Walsdorf Drug Store on Magazine Street and Napoleon Avenue) had a party for her twentieth birthday. Dora begged to go to the rented hall for the party; he not only allowed it, but gave his permission for her and her brothers and sisters to use the family's Stanley Steamer for their transportation. When the dance ended and the Geiseler children tried to leave in the family car, it would not budge. Attired in their evening gowns and tuxedos, they pushed the Stanley Steamer all the way to their home, only to be met by a worried father, who demanded, "What's the reason for your coming home late?" The Geiseler children had enough evidence—their fatigue and dusty, gritty appearance—to satisfy their father.

The Geiseler home on Calliope and Clio Streets had parental rules which the children more or less followed. Since their stern father also had a soft side, they were sometimes able to convince him to bend the rules, as in the case of the Walsdorf birthday dance. Nonetheless, Dora remembers some unbendable rules:

Everything had to be proper—dress, manners, and behavior.

Everybody went to church (although Jenni occasionally "ragged up" her piano playing when she played for church services).

The girls were not allowed to make loud noises out of doors.

The girls could not play in the street—this was not ladylike.

The Geiseler home was a happy growing-up place for Dora. She and her family laughed freely. The saddest event in her life was the time when her brothers Charlie and Joe were inducted into the Army in 1914. Fortunately, they returned to New Orleans safely after World War I, and the Geiseler family resumed their zest for life. Although she has never married, her memories from her family of origin and her extended family's warm support provide Dora Geiseler with a broad smile and readiness for a hearty laugh.

PaPoose Root Beer

Ideas come from a variety of sources. They can be the result of necessity, human experience, or just esoteric sources, like a vision. According to Emile Zatarain, Sr., his root beer extract trademark came to him that way. He saw a vision of a white papoose and decided to use it as the trademark for his newly created beverage.

His company was originally known as PaPoose Products Company in 1889. The name was eventually changed to Zatarain's. Prior to World War I, the Zatarain Company carried a variety of grocery products, such as bluing, bleach, spices, and coffee. The company had direct store delivery throughout the New Orleans area, going directly to Winn Dixie stores to contract with individual managers. A change occurred in 1968 when the company changed to a broker network. Direct sales were eliminated, and the company began to sell to chain stores and warehouses. Zatarain products were originally sold only in Houma, Thibodaux, and New Orleans, and had limited sales in Baton Rouge. With later expansion, the sales force expanded into Mississippi, Alabama, and Texas.

The Zatarain family sold its interest in the business in 1963 and the company was moved from Valmont Street in uptown New Orleans to 82 First Street in Gretna. Zatarain, Inc. is now owned by Westpath Equities, Ltd., whose headquarters is located in Chicago.

Since 1960 the company's president and chief executive officer has been Chloe Anderson. She oversees the work of eighty employees: the vice president of marketing; plant manager; director of research and development; a sales force of five; an office staff of six; five warehouse employees; and four truck drivers. The remaining fifty-seven employees mix and package the 170 different items, including crab boil, breadings, creole mixes, and creole mustard.

Chloe is definitely in control of Zatarain's, Inc. As we were going through the production section, I observed some boxes of spices clogged on the conveyor belt. She stopped, bent over, and broke the logjam; we then proceeded with our tour.

Where did this chief executive officer come from? She was born to Joe and Evie Russell in Kosciusko, Mississippi. When she was in the fifth grade, her family moved to Benoit, Mississippi, a small town located near the Mississippi River, upstream from the Crescent City (Benoit was at one time closer to the river than it is now, before the river changed its course).

Benoit is an agricultural town and its residents know about and cater to cotton and soybean farmers; encourage deer and turkey hunting along the river side of the Mississippi River levee; and invite fishermen to catch catfish, bass, croppie, and bream in the Oxbow Lake, created by the river's change of course. The community church serves as the meeting place for Presbyterians, Baptists, and Methodists. As a developing girl, Chloe was influenced by all of the above realities. After graduation from Benoit High School, Chloe spent one year at the Mississippi State College for Women in Columbus before attending and being graduated from the University of Kentucky.

Chloe moved downstream to become a resident of New Orleans thirty-seven years ago. Before joining Zatarain's, she worked as a manager at a company which sold both bakery equipment and baking mixes (Charles P. Wagner and Brothers). Being a woman and a president of a corporation was not a commonly found combination in the 1960s; it isn't all that common in the 1990s. Reflecting on her presidency in 1960, I expected Chloe to say that being a female executive officer was unusual and that she met resistance from her male counterparts. Quite to the contrary, she said, "Men who were suppliers and corporate executives helped me and were even more tolerant of my mistakes than females would have been." As far as special feelings of accomplishment, "I was too busy being president of a company and being a wife and mother of one son to give much thought to my being female."

The Way It Was

Everyone and everything changes, although sometimes the changes occur so slowly they are almost imperceptible. That could be said of Hubig's Pies and Henry Anthony Barrett, its Chief Executive Officer. Henry subscribes to the axiom, "If it ain't broke, don't fix it." Notwithstanding his white hair, even Henry's appearance has hardly changed since he and Albert Buiegan, his original partner, bought the pie business in 1953. His tall, erect frame and alert mind belie his age, which is over ninety.

Hubig's business office looks much the way it did decades ago, with low ceilings and pine paneling on the walls. The four-room suite is located on the second floor, above the shop area, at 2417 Dauphine Street. Two of the rooms—a veritable beehive of activity—are where telephone calls, bookkeeping, payments, and administrative matters are handled. (It was here that I saw one noticeable concession to change, the addition of a computer; it was not surprising to learn that the CEO neither recommended nor approved it.) The checkup room is where the fifteen routemen balance their accounts for the day. The room contains wooden pigeonhole compartments, where each routeman deposits his daily receipts and picks up his orders from Hubig's business associates, Otto ("Toby") Ramsey, Jr., Thomas Lamar Bowman, and Mike Tricou.

The executive office, shared by Henry and Toby, is testimony to Henry's philosophy that, "Fancy offices don't make profit." No changes have been made to the office since at least 1953. The back-to-back desks are cluttered with what appeared to be an accumulation of nearly forty years of paperwork. I noticed a pair of shoes lying on a chair, and inquired, "Are these your shoes, Mr. Barrett?" "No, they're Toby's." He looked at Toby's desk and smiled, "I've tried to get him to clean it up." As Toby and I looked at Henry's desk, piled with magazines, newspapers, and a collection of other unrelated materials, I recalled an old saying about the pot calling the kettle black.

Hubig's shop area, where pies are baked, wrapped, and boxed, also seems to be about the same as it was years ago. It is fascinating to walk through the five thousand square feet of pie-making activity, watching the veteran employees weigh, measure, and mix the ingredients; prepare the fillings; hand shape the dough; use an old peel blade to insert the pies into and remove them from the two rotating ovens; catch the pies as they come off the cooling rack after being baked in the traveling oven; and pack them for delivery. Many of the sixty-five to seventy-five employees have been around for decades. There is no compulsory retirement age, so the employees may work as long as they choose. Henry briefly comments, "We don't fire and hire like some companies."

The recipes (not publicized) for Hubig's pies—apple (Henry's favorite), cherry, lemon, peach, pineapple, and sweet potato—are the same as they were decades ago. The routemen and six brokers distribute Hubig Pies in and around New Orleans and as far as Lafayette. According to Henry, advertising is a waste of money because customers know about Hubig Pies and competition comes and goes. Most, however, have gone. Henry's first partner, Albert Buiegan, introduced sliced cake and also tried to expand the business to the Mississippi Gulf Coast. Neither the cake nor the expanded territory were successful. According to Henry, "We left it the way it was and cut out that foolishness."

The Henry Barrett-Hubig Pie story isn't likely to change, although Henry admits that his three junior partners may decide to make some changes when he is no longer on the pie-making scene. Then again, they may decide it's best not to tamper with over fifty years of success.

Ding-Dong Momma

Clearing the forests, burning the stumps, cultivating the land, hunting for any wild animal afoot, and fishing for anything that swam. That was the wilderness life that Alice North Cannon knew as a girl growing up at Laurel Hill in West Feliciana Parish. Her nearest neighbor was ten miles away, but she says she managed to complete "thirteen grades" in school. Her English father taught her that the world can "kill and eat you, but they can't take your education away from you."

The Crescent City lured Alice from West Feliciana wilderness living. She worked as a soda jerk at the Katz and Besthoff Drug Store on the corner of South Carrollton and South Claiborne Avenues for three years. She changed jobs in 1943 when the opportunity to make eighty-eight cents an hour collecting fares on the streetcar—seven cents per passenger—was too much to resist. While riding "wherever eight wheels [the streetcar] took me," she became known as the "Ding-Dong Momma," because of the streetcar bell that she rang. Alice says that as a "woman railroader," she was allowed to work until February 1946, "when the Johnnies came marching home."

After World War II Alice went to work for Binder's Bakery, making bread and pie shells, filling buns, and glazing doughnuts. In those days, pie shells were made and placed in a row of pans on a four-by-forty-foot table. A sheet of dough was placed over the pans that were lined up on a table; Alice pressed the dough by hand into pans and then trimmed the dough around the outer rim of each pan. She completed the pies by adding the filling with her hands. Binder's Bakery was her home for twenty years.

Over the years Alice has kept pace with change. Now age eighty-two, for the last twenty-two years she has clocked in at Hubig's Pies, where she has filled, sliced, wrapped, and boxed fruit pies. No longer quite the frontier person she was seventy years ago, she now sits in Hubig's lounge area where she affixes labels to pie boxes. With the agility of a twenty-year old, Alice methodically removes the self-adhesive labels from the backing and temporarily sticks them to her white uniform apron. After she has accumulated about a dozen labels, she puts them on the pie boxes. Her hands move rhythmically from roll, to apron, to box. Throughout the process, Alice's crisp, rapid speech never stops. As she works she greets her co-workers by name as they enter the lounge for a Coke or coffee break. She teases them and they affectionately call her "Old Gal."

Throughout her bakery career, Alice has always worn the same style of white dress and apron. Only once did she come to work out of uniform, shocking her co-workers by wearing a plaid "street dress"—the zipper in her uniform broke as she was getting dressed and her spare uniform was in the laundry.

The "old gal" had to take maternity leave at age sixty to deliver the last of her five children. She and her first husband, Earl Collins, had two children and she had three with her second husband, Joseph Wire Cannon (both husbands died of "natural causes"). Since I wanted to spell Joseph's middle name correctly, I asked if it were spelled W-I-R-E. "That's right—just plain old wire," she quickly responded.

When it comes to conveniences, Alice's life is Spartan. She lives in a shotgun house on France Street and uses the RTA busses to get to work, shopping, or wherever else she wants to go. When she is not working, she is making a "grocery garden, cleaning her house, running errands, or fishing."

"What do you do when you get all dressed up and go out?" I asked.

"I go fishing."

"What do you catch?"

"Anything that bites," she answered curtly.

"How long are you going to keep up this pace, Alice?"

"Another thirty years," she said unhesitatingly, then added, "I'll retire this year from Hubig's because they can't get insurance for me—but I'll find another job."

Although the years have taken a toll on her frame, she still stands five-feet-six-inches tall and weighs 165 pounds. She has never worn glasses because she sees everything she chooses. When I asked her the color of her eyes, she turned to me, eyed me without moving, and stated matter-of-factly, "Cat-eye color." As we talked, she stood to change her seated position and complained, "I don't like this sitting job. When they [the management] go home, I go in the back [the work area] and work."

Since I felt the trust level had built up sufficiently, I opted to ask her about her philosophy of life. Since she had been reared a Methodist, I expected her to respond in a "Methodical" way. I asked her about being home after a day's work at Hubig's. "Before I go to sleep, I think, what did I eat today? Whatever it was, I won't eat it tomorrow—it will be different. What did I do today? I won't do it tomorrow—it's got to be different too. I work on keeping my marbles rolling. Everything that happens to the body starts in the mind." I interrupted her philosophical discourse to ask, "Do you plan to marry again?" Not ruling it out completely, she pensively answered, "I don't think so." She continued in that mood, "I drink only coffee and tap water—never any ice water. The body is warm and needs warm drinks. Air conditioning is not good for people. I have only a fan. The good Lord gave us fresh air and I'm going to use it." I asked for one last philosophical statement. She looked at me mischievously, "I'm going to keep on raising hell!"

Bogalusa

A few miles north of Lake Pontchartrain in Washington Parish lies a paper mill town called Bogalusa. If the wind is blowing toward Highway 21, someone passing through may smell Bogalusa before seeing it.

Not everybody from the Washington Parish town chooses to remain there. Some elect to leave for reasons other than the odor of the mill. Anthony Saragusa was one of those persons. Born in Bogalusa in 1910; by 1919 he was living in New Orleans. Before he left his birth town, he had spent countless hours in the woods either swimming or picking crab apples, coon grapes, and muscadines. School neither attracted him nor held him. By the time he left Bogalusa, he had quit school without the advantage of learning to read or write. When he moved to the Crescent City, however, he did not totally leave behind his native town. He is called "Bogalusa Saragusa" in the French Market today.

While most twelve-year-old New Orleans boys had other interests, such as scouting, Tony loved to visit the French Market. Farmers packed the market to sell their produce, remaining for as many hours or days as it took for them to return home with empty wagons and full pockets. Tony was fascinated by the fisherman who sold fish and shrimp. He remembers that some sold their fish by bunches, rather than by the fish or the pound. Bogalusa strained his brain to remember the species of fish that merchants sold bunched together; within two minutes he recalled—mullet.

The vegetable vendors held a greater attraction for young Tony. He tended to stay on the Mint (Old U. S. Mint) end of the market. Since he had little to lose and a lot to gain, Tony would go out to the parishes that grew vegetables, buy them from the farmers, and bring them into the French Market for a meager return on his money. This enterprising effort was referred to as *speculation*.

The lure of the bucks tempted Tony to leave the French Market to work. The Dixie Iron Works on Tchoupitoulas Street was one of those places that seduced him. His love affair with the French Market, however, drew him back to the market. (The fact that he could not read a ruler also discouraged him from remaining with Dixie.) He knew strawberries, tomatoes, mustard greens, collards, watermelons, and pumpkins. He returned to the market to stay.

When he reached his seventies, Bogalusa had an opportunity to open a produce business of his own. Befriended by Mrs. Schenk (he does not know her first name), he was allowed to sell produce in her building on the river side of French Market Place. She gave him the first month's rent free and he stayed there from the early 1980s until 1990.

This vendor who may not have known his letters knew his produce and knew that he had to sell his products for more than he bought them. When he bought fruits and vegetables, he paid for them within twenty-four hours. If he sold a Number One tomato, it was exactly that—never a Number Two. He practiced honesty in his business, giving his customers what they paid for and telling them what they were getting. Bogalusa Saragusa ran a taut ship. He always wanted to have a quarter of a million dollars on which to retire. By the time he closed his doors on his produce market, the poor boy from Washington Parish had reached his goal.

At eighty-one, Bogalusa gets up and leaves his home when he wants to—no more rising at 4:00 A.M.

Whenever the urge strikes, he heads for the French Market. His destination is usually Fucci's Wholesale Fruit and Vegetable Market where he voluntarily packs and unpacks produce. As Bogalusa finished his unpaid work at the market, one of the owners said in my presence, "Bogalusa, do you want this?" Tony nodded and walked off with a nine-dollar box of California avocados. Before he loaded them into his car, he turned to give me the biggest of the avocados and said, "I'll give some of them to my neighbors."

Love Among the Tombs

It was a typical New Orleans afternoon: high humidity, ninety-five degrees Fahrenheit, and a threatening dark cloud overhead. I sat in my car, engine running, on Music Street between St. Roch Cemetery No. 1 and No. 2. The gate to No. 2 was open, but because the weather was becoming increasingly hostile, I contemplated whether I should leave or dash into the cemetery to find the person (unknown to me at the time) who cared for this home for the dead. Of all the cemeteries under the supervision of the Archdiocese of New Orleans, this was one of the most well maintained—obviously somebody cared.

I chose to leave. At that moment a man walked toward the entrance of St. Roch No. 2 and stood under an overhang to protect himself from the weather. It was Albert Warren Hattier, an employee of the cemetery for thirty-two years (for ten of those years he worked full time with the New Orleans Fire Department and part time for the cemetery). He retired in 1987, but after four years in retirement he returned to volunteer his services at the cemetery and continues working there today.

He has chosen not to marry, but instead to take care of his mother and grandparents, the George H. Perrots. The Perrots are buried in the family tomb in St. Roch No. 2. The impressive double-granite tomb, just inside the gate, is also reserved for both his and his mother's burials. It memorializes his grandfather George H. Perrot, a fireman for the New Orleans Fire Department, and sexton for the cemeteries from 1941 to 1953. The inscription under grandfather George's name reads:

FOR HIS DEVOTED SERVICE
TO THE PEOPLE OF
THIS COMMUNITY
AS SEXTON OF ST. ROCH CEMETERIES, 1941-1953

For the space he has reserved for himself, the inscription reads:

ALBERT W. HATTIER, JR.
GRANDSON OF GEORGE H. PERROT, SR.
A MAN WHO CARRIED OUT THE LEGACY
OF HIS GRANDFATHER AS SEXTON OF
ST. ROCH CEMETERIES, 1955-

Throughout the interview Albert had a natural smile as he talked possessively about the cemetery. His grandfather had devoted a part of his life to St. Roch No. 1 and No. 2, as did his uncles Louis and George Perrot. About his grandfather George, he recalled "old ladies" coming to the cemeteries to put flowers in the urns on their family members' graves. If they were unable to reach the flower containers, his grandfather would voluntarily get a ladder to reach the fourth tier and deposit the flowers for them. As a young boy assisting his grandfather, he sold buckets of sand for twenty cents each to family members who believed that fresh sand should cover the raised burial sites of their loved ones on All Saints' Day. Albert kept a dime per bucket for his services and gave the cemetery officials the balance. His smile broadened as he stated, "This is the only cemetery that has done this in the United States: I have gone to half—and will finish the other half—of the urns to drill a three-quarter-inch hole in each of them to prevent the water from collecting and freezing in the winter, causing the urns to burst."

As I strolled along the walks, each designated with appropriate names such as Little Flower of Jesus, St. Mary, St. Patrick, St. Vincent, and St. George (named for his grandfather), Albert's eyes were constantly scanning to detect work that needed to be done or anyone to whom he could offer assistance. He noticed that the cemetery employees were preparing a tomb on the third tier for a funeral the next day. Albert wanted me to peek inside. Kindly and respectfully, Albert requested that I be allowed to look in. Permission was granted. As an aside, Albert remarked, "I have respect for the feelings of all the family members whose dead are buried here."

As we passed along the walks, Albert related stories about Mrs. Fallon who was buried here, and Reverend William Himmrich who was buried there. A man was walking out carrying a broom and cleaning compounds. Albert flagged him down and introduced him, "This is Clyde Olsen. He comes here every week to clean his mother's tomb." He identified with Clyde as he reflected, "He chose not to marry and to look after his mother until she died four years ago. Now, he cares for her tomb."

As we stood between the cemeteries on Music Street, Albert shared unrelated anecdotes with me. He told me about, and later showed me, the chapel in St. Roch No. 1 which has a seven-by-seven-foot room adjacent to the altar which houses symbols representing healings. St. Roch, who died in 1327, effected miraculous cures through prayer and tender touches. Plaster of paris hands, legs, a section of an abdomen, a single breast, dolls, and crutches, hang on or lean against the wall. A statue of a kind, unidentified person stands alongside St. Lucy of the Eyes. In the Chapel of St. Roch No. 2 is a bas-relief of Jesus, donated by Arch Duane Sheffield.

According to Albert, when the donor went through financial hardships, he requested a refund on his donation. On the side of St. Roch No. 2, toward St. Roch Avenue, are unmarked graves for African Americans who were moved from their original places of burial to less desirable sites. Often the poor and unattended buried their dead at this cemetery. Albert related how neighborhood boys would have altercations on the playground, but would agree to settle their differences, demanding, "Meet me between the cemeteries." It was here on melodic Music Street, between the homes of the dead, that they resolved issues using fisticuffs.

Having an interest in the psychological makeup of Albert Hattier, I asked, "Why do you do what you do?" Without a moment's hesitation, Albert responded, "I love the people who come here, and want to serve them. I love St. Roch and want to take care of it." This explains the love among the tombs.

Son of a Watchmaker

It might be said that watchmakers *beget* only watchmakers. But, do they? From the marriage of native New Orleanians Christian Fischer and Margaretha Alexander in 1880 came eight boys and three girls. Not all of their offspring lived to adulthood and only the youngest son, Adolph Julius Fischer, survives today. Of the six sons who lived to adulthood, two were watchmakers, one was a jeweler, another was a conductor on a streetcar, and the fifth son was an elevator mechanic and sheet metal worker. The sixth, Adolph, had a variety of work experiences.

Like other growing-up lads, Adolph's work was his play. His environment on Danneel and Second Streets was not the most conducive for moral development in the early 1900s—there were barrooms on every corner. Adolph attests that the New Orleans police referred to his neighborhood as the "crime belt." Unlike today, in the early 1900s that meant a crime occurred every now and then.

Within a block of his home were shops which housed the meat market, the tailor, and the shoemaker. He played baseball and caught garfish in the New Basin Canal to sell to Greek restaurateurs for twenty-five cents apiece. On Sundays, he and his father walked from South Rampart Street to the Jackson Barracks, stopping along the way to buy a beer for father Christian and a cream soda for son Adolph. Fatigued by the walk to the Barracks, but refreshed by his soda, Adolph knew his father's statement was forthcoming, "What ya say, let's walk back."

Play was not always active. Adolph was often content just to observe the happenings on or near the Mississippi River. He watched the stevedores load and unload the ships, grunting and straining as they maneuvered dollies loaded with cargo from the docks to the ships. Watching the stevedores pushing and pulling fully loaded dollies up and down the steep ramps both fascinated and puzzled young Adolph—how were the men strong enough to do that? Occasionally barrel races were held on the Mississippi. At other times, flags were tied atop greased poles on the bows of the ships and prizes were offered to the contestants who could successfully climb the poles to retrieve the flags.

Adolph started working in order to be able to buy a nickel ticket to the theater or spend a nickel for a hamburger. In the next block from his home on Danneel Street, he negotiated for his first after-school job, running oyster orders from the oyster house to the customers' homes. Since clock making was in his background, he applied for and got a job as an engraver's apprentice with Arthur G. Shultz in the old Godchaux Clothing Store in the Central Business District. A dumbwaiter connected the upstairs workroom (where he worked) and the jewelry store on the first floor. Orders for engraving were received in the store downstairs and relayed to him upstairs via the dumbwaiter. During his lunch break one day Adolph caught a newborn mouse. He brought it back to work, packed it into one of the boxes used for his engraved work, and lowered it on the dumbwaiter. His mischievous plan was successful. A fragile female worker in the jewelry store opened it and fainted. Since Adolph was the only engraver on duty, his employer Mr. Schultz had to do only minimal sleuthing to identify the culprit.

He confronted and upbraided his young apprentice, but did not dismiss him. There were many reasons for his leniency, but chief among them was the fact that the young apprentice served as his courier to the horse track. Adolph quipped, "I learned as much about horse racing as I did engraving."

Adolph took a giant step to his next place of employment. He sought and gained employment on Magazine Street with the Koretby Machinist Shop. After he gave this vocation a try, he decided that the Cumberland Telephone Company was more attractive. He soon found out that shouldering and rolling heavy wire through weeds, mud, and water required excessive energy, so he chose to move on to a job with the federal government because it was less strenuous and offered more security. Adolph allotted the Veteran's Bureau at the Old U. S. Mint on Esplanade Avenue only five years of his life. What he recalls most about this period was not his veteran's work, but coaching the Bureau-sponsored girls' softball team. He didn't get paid for this avocation, but he didn't mind a bit.

Since his cousin was the head baker on a United Fruit Company ship, he signed on as a second baker. Who knows? Adolph might have ended his vocational search and been content with his Caribbean sailings. But as providence, fate, or whatever would have it, Adolph met Dorothy Augusta Vorbusch on a hayride while waiting for his next Caribbean assignment. Fred Mehrtens took Dottie to the hayride, but Adolph spotted her and this conversation ensued:

"Fred, you brought Dottie?"

"Yea, I did." responded Fred.

"Well, I'm going to take her home." announced Adolph confidently.

By October 24, 1928, Adolph had convinced Dottie to join him in a marriage which lasted for more than fifty years.

His next job "nearly cost him his pants." He

decided to buy his mother-in-law's grocery store on Prytania Street. The grocery stock consisted of a limited variety of groceries including "big ticket items" like ice cream and soft drinks. What kept him afloat during this segment of his multi-faceted career was his clandestine lottery business. He wrote lottery tickets for two or three years—at the same time the Reverend Munz was trying to get him to give it up to become a minister. Adolph left the grocery and lottery business, yearning to raise chickens in his backyard.

This wandering worker finally settled down as a patrolman for the Levy Board, the employment from which he retired at age sixty five. Retirement, however, did not mean monotony. Since the 1960s, Adolph's interests in hunting deer, gigging frogs, catching alligators, collecting coins, searching for Indian relics, and making children's toys have continued to fulfill his need for variety.

Dress Up for Canal Street

Ninety-five years to the day after her birth on January 13, 1896, Lola Weiss Lalande reflected on that special street called Canal Street, which historically divided the rowdy Americans from the sophisticates of the French Quarter.

It was always a special occasion when young Lola went to Canal Street. Maison Blanche, D. H. Holmes, Imperial Shoe Store, Coleman E. Adler Jewelers, and Hausmann's Jewelers drew New Orleans shoppers to this historic street. The dress code for her shopping outing was a Sunday dress with ruffles and lace over two cotton petticoats, along with a hat, veil, and gloves. She would not be allowed to wear any one of her six or eight school dresses for a Canal Street visit; nor would her school or play shoes have been considered appropriate. She always matched her hat with the Sunday shoes she wore. Reflecting on her childhood days at the beginning of the twentieth century, Lola mused, "I never thought Canal Street would change so."

Canal Street, along with all the other streets and places, has undergone some changes. From Lola's perspective, New Orleans is not the way it was. The streetcar on the Henry Clay and Coliseum line used to cost a nickel. The Tulane, Crescent, and Orpheum Theaters were legitimate, with productions like the "Merry Widow."

When an afternoon rain doused her Laurel Street neighborhood (her house was between Octavia and Joseph Streets), the dirt streets turned to mud—except a cobblestone street like Tchoupitoulas. The garbage was collected and deposited in open mule or horse-drawn carts. The lamplighters performed their ritual about dusk every evening. A nickel could buy a loaf of bread; shrimp were twenty-five cents for three pounds. The New Basin Canal was always open for her and her family to catch crawfish. There were no screens on the windows nor locks on the doors at her house. There was only an occasional crime—for instance, the Italian boy murdered in St. Bernard Parish. Newspaper hawkers went up and down the streets hollering, "Extra! Extra! Read all about it!" The scuttlebutt in the community alleged that he was killed by the Black Hand, a derogatory term referring to a Sicilian and Italian-American secret society engaged in criminal activity.

Her mother did the traditional housekeeping and cooking and her father was a detective for the New Orleans Police Department. Chickens ran freely in her backyard until it was time for Sunday dinner. The cistern next to her grayish-colored house caught rainwater for both bathing and drinking. (She loathed staying at her aunt's house because they used the same bath water for family baths. If she were third in line, it meant the two before her were more privileged than she.) The outhouse was a short distance from the backdoor. The fireplace burned coal and her mother cooked on a wood-burning stove in the kitchen. On cold evenings, her mother warmed a blanket for the foot of her bed. Birthdays offered her a choice of her favorite foods, such as chicken, veal, pork chops, and apple dumplings.

In addition to the influence of her home, the Salem Evangelical Church on Milan and Camp Streets impacted her young life. In her confirmation classes, she remembers Rally Day in October when the Sunday School rounded up all its members. Her first date occurred when a boy from Salem Church brought her home after a special church meeting. The church's influence also extended to her home. She remembers her mother Margaret singing religious songs as she sewed Lola's dresses: "Onward Christian Soldiers" and "What a Friend We Have in Jesus."

Playing hopscotch and blindman's bluff were Lola's outside games, while old maid cards kept her occupied inside. She remembered her first gold cross and her Kodak box camera. Public school teachers at McDonogh No. 14 on Jefferson Street taught the boys on one side of the room and the girls on the other. As a teenager, she won a trip to Panama for selling the most subscriptions to the *Times-Picayune*.

Among Lola's memories, going to Canal Street is one of her most special. It was her favorite thoroughfare. An outing there was always a "dress up" occasion.

The Art of Cupping

Anyone who is not associated with the coffee trade is likely to ask, "What is 'cupping' and why is it an art?" Earl Putnam Bartlett, Jr., has been in the coffee business for over fifty years, making him well qualified to answer the question. Cupping is the time-honored process in which sample coffee is tested by expert tasters to determine if the coffee is acceptable for purchase by the American Coffee Company for sale to retailers.

In 1941, Earl's father and George Dodge bought 85 percent of the stock in the American Coffee Company, whose history dated back to 1890. Before joining the Navy in World War II, Earl was a student at Tulane University during the regular sessions and worked at the Coffee Company during the summers. He was shifted from one phase of the business to another, working in roasting, shipping, and packing. He returned to the business after the war. By the time his father died in 1975, Earl had learned the ins and outs of the American Coffee Company, including "cupping."

The company purchases green coffee (unroasted beans) from Westfeldt Brothers, a New Orleans trading company whose suppliers are plantations in Central and South America. Samples of the green coffee beans are roasted, put in four-ounce cups, and covered with boiling water. As his father and his own experience has taught him, he visually observes the beans and then tastes the liquid, testing it for clarity, acidity, and body, to mention only a few of the tasting criteria. An order is placed for a shipment of coffee beans only after the cupping test meets Earl's exacting standards.

The sacks of green coffee are stored on the second floor of the American Coffee building at 800 Magazine Street. From there it is transferred to the third floor for the blending and roasting processes. Four roasters accommodate 132 bags at a time and one smaller Probat roaster is used to roast a twenty-five-pound bag of coffee for their gourmet line.

Chicory, a carrot-like vegetable root from France, is ground and added to the coffee during the roasting process (the chicory leaves, called endives, are used in salads). This important ingredient is added to the coffee to improve the flavor. Earl also maintains that chicory may even have medicinal value, benefitting the digestive process.

Housed on the first floor are the packing and shipping departments where French Market Coffee and Chicory is prepared for shipment. Coffee going to restaurants carries the Alameda label, and for the New Orleans retail market, American Coffee packages its products using the Union label.

Stepping off Magazine Street into the American Coffee Company building is like walking into the nineteenth century. The furnishings, equipment, and worn oak floors predate seventy-year-old Earl Bartlett. The desktop computers serve as the only reminders of the 1990s. Like his father before him, Earl's focus is on quality. Although the blends remain a well-guarded family secret, the quality is advertised and well-known to coffee drinkers. There's no need to change anything; it met the criteria of Earl's father and satisfied the palates of his customers. Earl continues to be satisfied with the taste and quality of French Market Coffee and Chicory and admits that he would be pleased if his son Fraser would continue the American Coffee Company tradition into the twenty-first century.

The Vegetable Man

On his winding vegetable and fruit route, Joseph Kaufman was known by various titles. He was "Brother Kaufman" to his customers who also knew him at the Greater Saint Stephen Baptist Church and "Mr. Kaufman" to those who did not. To those who didn't know him personally, he was simply the "Vegetable Man." Although his produce also included fruit, he never wanted to be called the "Fruit Man."

The environs of St. Francisville shaped Joseph for his first twelve years. His religious and moral teachings were translated into simple, practical living—no handcuffs or jail time for him. His father died when he was a baby. His mother, who made a living as a domestic, taught him to love God and respect his parents. Each of her six children recognized right and lived it.

Joseph came to New Orleans in 1929 when he was twelve, joining his mother who had come earlier to look for work. His life while living at 1152 Constance Street was typical of the 1920s. There were no busses; streetcars transported passengers anywhere in the city for a nickel. He remembers when transportation costs were hiked to an exorbitant seven cents. To Joseph, the Tenth Ward was a "beautiful place to live." The Irish Channel boys felt secure playing in the street. Joseph and his friends shot marbles, using large agatoid shooters—called "agates" or "tars"—to hit the other players' marbles and knock them out of a circle drawn in the dirt. When Joseph and his friends tired of routine marble games, they played a rougher game of shooting at each other's knuckles with the marbles—a strange but pleasurable pastime for the young boys. The retired eighty-two-year-old vegetable man reflected on his growing-up days, "There was hardly any crime." Lifting his hand, he continued, "I could hold up one hand numbering the crimes I remember and have some fingers left."

For a couple of years Joseph attended McDonogh No. 35 School from 7:30 to 9:30 P.M., Monday through Friday. His mother's need for support, coupled with his work ethic, motivated him to work for a blacksmith's shop on Magazine Street during the day, where he was paid fifty cents a day to lead the horses to be shod. He left the heat of the blacksmith's shop to work at the Casteix Drug Store. He then did a stint in the Merchant Marines with the United Fruit Company. By 1932 Joseph had married his first wife Mary. The necessity for work increased with the births of their four sons. Touro Infirmary provided employment for him until he shipped out to fight in World War II. His marriage to Mary ended when she chose to return to Baton Rouge to live closer to her mother.

He returned to the Crescent City after the war, married Leona, and began to sell fruits and vegetables from a pushcart in the Gentilly area. He purchased his produce from the French Market. If his stock needed to be replenished during the day, he shut down his cart and returned to the wholesale market to purchase more.

Joseph gradually expanded his business. For $175 he bought a Model A Ford truck to do his buying and used the tailgate to do his selling. Although he never bought a new truck, he continually upgraded. He replaced his Model A Ford with a 1947 Dodge, then a 1951 Chevrolet, a 1953 Ford, and finally a 1960 one-half-ton Apache truck. He changed his route whenever necessary to increase his sales. The six-day route went from North Robertson to Baronne Streets and from Martin

Luther King Boulevard to Fourth Street. He made three stops per block, calling out loudly at each stop, "Vegetable Man! Vegetable Man! I got tomatoes, apples, oranges, and mustard greens!" To make sure that no one missed him, his customers would telephone their neighbors in the next block to inform them, "He's on his way."

Joseph's customers counted on his promptness—for instance, they knew that at 3:30 P.M., he would be at South Liberty and First Streets. They also knew they would always get lagniappe. If they bought six bananas, the Vegetable Man threw in another one or two. If his produce stayed on his truck beyond a day, his prices dropped. Women delayed preparing their suppers until he came along, knowing they could depend on him to have fresh produce. The children were especially fond of him. Once he casually told a child on his route that he would return to play with him. The child's mother later reproved Joseph, "Don't ever say you're going to do anything with my child because he will believe you. He did not want to go to sleep until you came back to play with him."

During the early 1960s, the Vegetable Man worked six days a week, taking off only on Sundays for church. He started taking off on Mondays as well during the fifteen years prior to his retirement in 1983 after a heart attack. Only twice until he retired was Joseph the victim of a crime. In 1975 on Dryades and Second Streets, he was selecting a watermelon for a customer when a young man came up from behind him, slipped his hand into Joseph's pocket, and made off with $125. He excitedly called Leona to report what had happened:

"Did he [the robber] get hurt?" she asked.

"No," he replied

"Did you get hurt?" she continued to question.

"No," he responded.

"Then, forget it," she said philosophically.

A few days later on Danneel Street, Joseph was again busy selling when a young man aimed a pistol at him and demanded his money. The holdup man grabbed the cash that Joseph was holding between his fingers (a method of holding money developed in his early years as a gambler). The thief started running, but turned and fired at Joseph from about thirty-five feet away. He missed. It was not Joseph Kaufman's time.

His customers and his business were "beautiful,"—the Vegetable Man's favorite adjective. Other than the two thieves, everybody else was "beautiful." His church has always been special to Deacon Kaufman. Since Pastor Paul Sylvester Morton was always around the church doing something, Deacon Kaufman would pass by, leaving a bag of fruit for him. One day in 1979 Pastor Morton ventured, "You're getting mature. Come to work for the church." In 1985, he began work as a "supervisor" for the church. Today the Vegetable Man continues to meet "beautiful people." He no longer has to go to them—he's greeting them at the door of the Greater Saint Stephen's Baptist Church.

Where Martin Meets Higgins

Martin Barcelona and Herbert Higgins came together for a common purpose in 1955: the establishment of Martin & Higgins Jewelers at 4347 Chef Menteur Highway. Their entrepreneurial venture began when the two thirty-one-year-old jewelers decided to sell watches and rings one Christmas season. Their success at this venture, a joint profit of $900, encouraged them to open their own store. With an additional investment of $2000 each, they paid an advance on their leased retail space, built their showcases in Martin's garage, and hired watchmaker Ted Legendre. Herbert handled the sales in the front showroom and Martin crafted and repaired jewelry in the rear workroom.

Martin had worked for Coleman Adler and Roberts Jewelry and both he and Herbert had worked for White Bros. Jewelers. They were reared in New Orleans and brought more than just experience to their new business; they brought their reputations as trusted retailers as well. Their objective was to serve their customers and make a profit while maintaining the highest standards of business integrity. They pledged fairness and good craftsmanship to their customers—deception or dishonesty were not their *modus operandi.*

Over the years I have often been a customer at Martin & Higgins. It's not uncommon for them to tell me, "No charge" when I've attempted to pay for adjustments to my watch, or to charge me less than five dollars for minor repairs when they could have easily charged twenty. In addition to consistently being satisfied with the workmanship, service, and prices, I am amazed by the trust shown toward their customers. Unlike most jewelry stores today, they will place a piece of jewelry on the counter and allow the customer to examine it unattended.

Since making their initial investment, they have never had to borrow any additional money for their business. Their sales practices are not like those of other retail outlets. A clearance sale of any kind, such as a going-out-of-business sale or year-end sale, is unheard of at Martin & Higgins Jewelers. *Advertising* is not in their vocabulary. In over thirty-six years of service, Martin and Herbert can recall only two dissatisfied customers. They prefer to remember the long list of New Orleans notables that they have served over the years. Herbert discretely refused to reveal their names, but couldn't resist disclosing the fact that they made necklaces for television's Laverne and Shirley for an Endymion parade.

Not all of Martin & Higgin's clientele are among the notables. Herbert recalled a humorous event which had occurred just a few weeks before. An older teenager came to Martin & Higgins to select a set of wedding rings. He paid a down payment on the rings, and agreed to pick them up when the $150 balance was paid. Herbert asked him when his wedding was to be. "Tonight," he responded. "What are you going to do for rings?" Herbert asked. He shrugged, "Promise to give them to her when they are paid off." Herbert told the young man to take the rings and pay the balance later. Elated, the groom-to-be offered Herbert a slice of his wedding cake, which was outside in his car. Herbert thanked him but declined his generous offer. "Will he pay you the balance?" I asked. Herbert responded confidently, "Oh, yes, he'll pay."

Martin & Higgins Jewelers was originally located in the Gentilly Woods Shopping Center, the first shopping center in New Orleans. As larger malls opened in the area, Maison Blanche, Sears, and most of the smaller businesses eventually closed or moved to other locations. The partners decided to relocate to the Lela Building across the street. Considering some of the negative changes in the neighborhood, I asked Herbert if the store had ever been robbed, expecting him not only to say "yes," but to name a high number of incidents. Surprisingly, he said there's been only one holdup. Even more surprising, the front door of the store is not secured by an electronically controlled locking device seen so often today on retail establishments. "Herb, how do you account for this?", I asked. "We know all the people around here and we trust them."

Martin has retired and Herbert is now the sole owner of the business. When asked what he would change, Herbert reflected and said quietly, "Nothing, except a possible earlier relocation." At age sixty-seven, Herbert, who is married to the former Irma Sconca, is content to continue working indefinitely.

It's been over thirty-six years since the two young World War II veterans started out, hoping their business would survive. They succeeded financially; but more importantly, Martin & Higgins Jewelers has become a trusted, respected name synonymous with the Gentilly area.

Never too Late

Located on Old Gentilly Road at Chef Menteur Highway is the Lampe Gallery. The store-front sign advertises custom framing, mirrors, restorations, prints, and art supplies. The sign, however, is a bit misleading, for the Lampe Gallery offers far more. After customers ring the security bell and gain admission, they are greeted by either June or Frederick ("Fritz") Lampe, the proprietors and congenial hosts.

Their subdued, but genuine, friendliness may be characteristic of their South Dakota upbringing or just their reserved personality traits. With time and a few cups of CDM coffee, both Fritz and June opened themselves up to me. Historically, they passed each other in the high school halls in Huron, South Dakota; within two years after their graduations, Fritz Lampe and June Bowen were married. For twenty-eight years they remained in South Dakota where Fritz and other family members operated a grocery store, appropriately called Lampe Market. Before and after the births of daughters Barbara and Debbie, June maintained her interest in and practice of the old masters' techniques of painting with oils. Her Uncle Frank Freeland had taught her the techniques and instilled in her the love for this artistic expression while she was growing up in Dowagiac, Michigan.

When the Lampe Market was sold, Fritz and June

headed south for Houston, Texas, where he invested in a business selling nuts and bolts. It was through marketing for this business that the Lampes eventually migrated to New Orleans in 1958. Investments have a way of booming or busting; Fritz's business took the latter route. In New Orleans Fritz turned to mortgage banking and later to real estate before they were interviewed by Ed Means, the owner of Means Fine Arts and the heir to valuable paintings and nineteen thousand prints. Ed hired them both—June to restore paintings and Fritz to frame prints and paintings.

By 1968, Ed Means was committed to either selling his art business or locking its doors. Fritz and June, then in their fifties, picked up the option to buy Means Fine Arts on Old Gentilly Road, renaming it the Lampe Gallery. Was it too late for this middle-aged couple to start a new venture? Creativity and energy level told them, "It's never too late." The Lampes were energized to set new goals while fulfilling already established ones.

June teaches talented and motivated art students from areas extending both east and west on the Gulf Coast. According to June, each class day brings a different family of art students. The class on Mondays studies and practices art while enjoying special goodies from a Picayune, Mississippi, student. On Tuesdays, the class brings prepared dishes for lunch. The Saturday class ends each session with a taste of sherry. The other classes have less social structure, but will have some seasonal specialty, such as a King Cake. These are June's friends as well as her students.

When she was in her mid-sixties, June was challenged by one of her students to experiment with encaustic painting, an ancient method used by the Greeks, Romans, and Egyptians. The student's insistence mildly irritated June, but it also nudged her to research the art style and to experiment with it. Using melted beeswax containing pigment as its chief ingredient, June learned to apply heat to create images of persons and things in her revived art form. Hanging on their studio wall is an encaustic painting entitled "Faces of Eve" which is thirty-by-eighty-four inches. Not even June is certain about the number of Eve's faces in the painting. Only one face and body is obvious—the others have to be discovered. "Perhaps," June reflects as she glances at the painting, "there are as many as a baker's dozen." About this medium she muses, "I bring sculptural feelings to my painting, since this medium lends itself to the buildup without any loss of its intrinsically lustrous qualities." Her encaustic paintings have been shown in art shows on the West Coast, winning coveted awards.

About ten years ago, Fritz added a dimension to his framing and general managing of the Lampe Gallery. The classified section in the *Times-Picayune* carried an advertisement for the sale of carousel horses. At June's insistence (and against all the traffic odds), June and Fritz followed up on the ad, which led to a West Bank motel where they found and eventually purchased a C. W. Parker carousel horse. The vintage 1912 horse needed restoration desperately: three legs were missing, most of the tail had been broken off, and only stubs remained where the ears had been. Since the Parker carousel horse was an assemblage of wooden planks laminated together, restoration was more than just wood carving. The horse was stripped of layers of paint; clamps were used to hold the glued pieces of wood together; the parts were carved; and the tail was fitted to the body. Wood filler, dowels for reinforcement, paint, sanding, and finally buffing with steel wool produced a C.W. Parker as genuine as the original Leavenworth, Kansas, Product Number 35.

Now in their mid-seventies, Fritz and June Lampe are still dreaming. Fritz's dreams include restoration of carousel animals along with his artistic framing. June dreams of an art show in New York City and creating a life-size bronze sculpture. When is it too late? From their points of view, *never*.

Mighty Mouse and
George Washington

This is a strange combination of the fictional and the real. Mighty Mouse belongs to the world of cartoons, and every informed person identifies George Washington with the presidency of the United States and cherry trees, among other things.

What's the connection between a cartoon character and the first president? The answer to half of the question came early in my interview with Mary Roeder Russell and her husband Emanuel Absolom Russell. In stark contrast to Emanuel, who has been slowed down by hip replacement surgery, Mary is energetic and hyperactive. Her husband refers to her as Mighty Mouse.

Answering the Washington question involves getting to know a little more about Mary Roeder Russell. She was born in Shreveport, Louisiana; moved with her parents (her father was an executive with Gulf Oil) to Texas and Mexico; and then came to the New Orleans area (Avondale) to work as a telephone operator for the Southern Pacific Railroad. One of the calls she received on the switchboard was from Emanuel Absolom Russell, an employee of Louisville and Nashville (L&N) Railroad. Emanuel's official calls led to an unofficial one in which he invited Mary to accompany him to a Mardi Gras parade. Their date eventually led to their paying a twenty-five-dollar fee to a minister and a lifetime commitment.

Their first apartment was located in Algiers on

Verret Street across from the Whitney Bank. The newly-weds were attracted to the apartment by the floral lino-leum rugs and especially by the low rent. Like other aspiring couples, they eventually chose to "move up." Their next residence, a former servants' quarters on Bour-bon Street, had a good view from the balcony, but little else—there was no hot water, no kitchen cabinets, and no lockers (closets) for their clothes. From Bourbon Street, they moved to Clematis Street before buying a house at 8720 Chef Menteur, where they lived far enough from the heart of the city to raise chickens and turkeys. They sold the eggs for twenty cents a dozen and processed twenty to twenty-five turkeys and chickens on the weekends. Living far out on Chef Menteur, however, also exposed them to hobos looking for handouts and gypsies who stole their poultry one night as they slept. Emanuel and Mary moved to a more established neighborhood on Mor-rison Road, where noise was not allowed before 7:00 A.M. or after 11:00 P.M.

While living on Morrison Road, Mary's interest in painting dinner plates prompted her to call the Lampe Gallery on Gentilly Boulevard to request lessons from artist and co-owner June Lampe. June could not assist her with painting plates; but offered to help her with oil painting instead. Under June Lampe's tutelage, Mary completed her first oil painting—a landscape—in 1970. As she progressed in painting with oils, her interest shifted to portrait painting.

Mary's portrait painting answers the question about George Washington. She was a member of the Order of the Eastern Star and Emanuel was a member of the Masonic Order. She selected George Washington as the subject of her first portrait because he was the first Grand Master for the State of Virginia. The portrait, com-pleted in 1972, is of Washington in a standing position, almost life-size. Mary had it framed and presented it to the Sun Masonic Lodge 336F&AM in Sun, Louisiana. Since painting her first portrait of George Washington,

Mary the Mighty Mouse has painted and framed fifty-five portraits of Washington and presented them to various Masonic lodges in Florida, Mississippi, and Louisiana.

Twenty years ago Mary and Emanuel decided to buy property and build a house in Hickory, Louisiana (Mary continued to commute to the Crescent City for her insurance work until 1991). This was the first time Emanuel had ever lived outside of New Orleans—he had never even been to Uptown New Orleans before he met Mary. He used to call her a "Yankee" because she was born in Shreveport—north of Baton Rouge.

It may not be accurate to call her a Yankee, but Mighty Mouse definitely suits her. She built two houses on the Hickory property; maintains them because of her husband's physical limitations; feeds and takes care of two hundred ducks and six dogs; and continues painting portraits of George Washington.

Downstream and Upstream

Quietly and expertly the MV *Senator T. Stumpf* ferryboat docks on Canal Street to load both passengers and vehicles for a trip downstream to Algiers. The trucks and automobiles are parked in rows on the vehicular deck, while up to 1700 passengers sit or stand on the passenger deck or the upper deck, referred to as the Texas deck.

Obviously the ferryboat that operates between the east and west banks of the Mississippi River does not navigate on its own or even by computer. In the wheelhouse for the afternoon and evening shift is Captain Fred Morris Trowbridge. With skilled hands and watchful eyes, Captain Trowbridge controls the levers, the flanking and the back rudders levers.

It was on a humid August evening when I boarded the ferryboat for the trip to Algiers and back. Since I was in a vehicle, the cost was a dollar—passengers are transported free. As I chatted with a deckhand, I asked about the captain who was operating the ferryboat. Although it was not permissible, the deckhand encouraged me to climb the ladder to the wheelhouse for an introduction to Captain Trowbridge. As I opened the door to the ladder housing, darkness was all I saw and a deep commanding voice was all I heard: "You are entering the wrong door. Please close it and leave." Somewhat intimidated, I paused momentarily, but asked permission to climb the ladder. Permission was granted. This was my first introduction to Captain Trowbridge. The captain stood as erect as possible because of an old back injury while manipulating the levers before him. With precision, he negotiated the ferryboat into position. In spite of the strong current of the Mississippi River, he docked the ferryboat at the foot of Canal Street without the slightest bump—like putting a baby in a cradle. As he maneuvered the ferryboat, he explained each procedure to me.

Since December 8, 1977, Captain Trowbridge has repeated this navigational process. Only once has he been involved in an accident on the river. Three connected barges were being pushed upriver; the tugboat captain chose to navigate near Algiers Landing because of high water and an approaching ship; the barges rammed the stern of Captain Trowbridge's ferryboat. Fortunately, there were no personal injuries and only minimal structural damage.

Fred was born in a house on the corner of Amelia and Magazine Streets, just a few blocks from the river. His father Oliver worked on the river, serving as a captain for the Federal Barge Line. Fred's developing years were spent in the Gentilly area; but he was never far from either Lake Pontchartrain or the Mississippi River.

As a teenager, he worked for Mr. Konns, who was employed by Logeno and Collins who had a lease on the filled-in land from the Industrial Canal to the New Basin Canal. Mr. Konns got the lease because he was the only one who knew how to grow grass on the pumped-in soil to prevent soil erosion. Young Fred worked with Mr. Konns as a helper with the company's cows and horses which grazed on the grassy stretch of land. To commute to and from his work, Fred often rode the train (the Pontchartrain Railroad) which ran along Elysian Fields Avenue from the river to the lake. The train's engine was called *Smoky Mary* because of the thick black smoke produced by the soft coal that it burned.

During World War II he was assigned to a Navy torpedo patrol boat. From the time of his military discharge until his present employment as a ferryboat captain with the State of Louisiana, he has continued to work on or near the water.

From early afternoon until the last ferryboat runs in the evening, Captain Fred Trowbridge, along with his four deckhands, transports vehicles and passengers from one side of the river to the other. The vehicular passengers are commuters, wanting only to get to the other side, while many of the pedestrians are tourists, seeking the exhilaration of riding back and forth across the Mississippi River.

Lucky Dogs

Each morning eighteen to twenty-three people enter the building at 517 Gravier Street. They are Lucky Dog vendors, requisitioning their supplies for the day. They egress dressed in red-and-white striped smocks and matching baseball-type caps, pushing carts designed to look like their marketed product—hot dogs.

Hot dog cart? It is just that by design—a large aluminum bun and mustard-covered wiener on wheels with a red hood mounted above the metal bun to house the hot dog steamer and a shelf for the buns. A rectangular metal box attached to the rear of the cart is the storage unit for CO_2, H_2O, and whatever else is needed for the one-person operation. Painted on the unit is the unofficial New Orleans symbol, the *fleur-de-lis*, and the words, "New Orleans Tradition since 1948."

Lucky Dogs management provides the jumbo and regular hot dogs and sausage links with an equal number of buns; a tank of Pepsi Cola; and the basic condiments, chili, mustard, and onions. The vendors are responsible for catsup, jalapeño peppers, sauerkraut, and spicy mustard. When the working day ends, the vendors pay the Lucky Dogs management 84 percent of the sales for the day, keeping 16 percent for themselves, plus tips.

Among the vendors on any given workday are Chet and Maggie Anderson. Chet's starting inventory includes 108 jumbo and twelve regular hot dogs, eighteen sausage links, and a tank of Pepsi. He pushes his giant hot dog cart toward the Mississippi River to the Convention Center. Following Chet is his wife Maggie, her cart loaded with fifty-four jumbo and thirty-six regular hot dogs, nine sausage links, and a supply of Pepsi. Maggie's clientele is different from Chet's; she parks her cart near the Aquarium of the Americas, where hungry children file in and out.

In 1984 Chet and Maggie responded to a *Times-Picayune* help-wanted advertisement submitted by Lucky Dogs. Since Chet had retired from the United States Army with a pension and medical benefits, he and Maggie wanted non-stressful jobs which allowed them to take time off to visit Las Vegas or their eleven children living in Texas and Indiana. They liked what the Lucky Dogs management described; thus, the Andersons embarked on a new career.

Following the Lucky Dogs tradition, Chet and Maggie sit or stand at their assigned locations—never hawking their merchandise, but waiting for their potential customers to have a hot dog and/or a Pepsi attack. They, along with their twenty or more vending colleagues, are scattered throughout the French Quarter and Warehouse District selling Lucky Dogs loaded with chili, onions, mustard, or the condiments of choice; making change for a motorist who needs to feed a parking meter; or guiding a bewildered tourist who wants to find Bourbon Street. Being at their locations from 10:30 A.M. until 7:00 P.M. can be a strain on their anatomies. If Chet or Maggie want a break, they close the hood and walk away. If they decide that they themselves have eaten enough hot dogs, they close up for a change-of-pace meal.

Like any other business, *the customer is always right,* and *courtesy* for Chet and Maggie is the rule of their working day. However, when rude customers push ahead of others, the Andersons find it difficult, if not impossible, to observe the maxim that the customer is *always* right. Regardless of the occasional negative stress, the Andersons intend to continue reporting each morning to 517 Gravier Street—the home of Lucky Dogs.

Beignets and Café au Lait?

No matter how many times some persons come to New Orleans—for whatever reason, business or pleasure—most guests do not feel that they have been to the Crescent City unless they have made at least one visit to the Café Du Monde, the Original French Market Coffee Stand. Since 1863 this coffee stand has served customers who wanted a quick lift, a settling of the shakes, or a gustatory delight of coffee with chicory, the ground root of a perennial plant with bright blue flowers.

Since 1945, visitors to the Big Easy who have made the requisite pilgrimage to the Café Du Monde have been served by petite Mary Graff Alexander. During her first seventeen years, Mary was a waitress, serving customers their orders of beignets—prepared from a secret recipe—and deliciously blended and brewed café au lait or café without milk. Mary was then stationed at the cash register, and has been a cashier at the Café Du Monde ever since.

Mary's growing-up years were spent at 409 Henry Clay Avenue. Her home was near Audubon Park, where her father, Theodore Graff, operated the carousel. With a warm smile she says, "I was reared on flying horses." Necessity required her to work and her energy allowed her to do it. By the time she was fourteen, little Mary was working at Pontchartrain Beach doing odd jobs after school and during the summers. During the winters, she cleaned school rooms, earning twenty-five cents for a classroom and ten cents per cloakroom. She worked in private homes, perspiring as she washed, ironed, and stretched curtains for one dollar and fifty cents a day.

The Big War opened up the job market for Mary. She was asked to apply as a waitress at the coffee stand in the French Market only because the men waiters had gone to war. Until the 1980s, when she retired from full-time work, her hours were very long. She originally worked the shift from 5:00 P.M. to 2:00 A.M. because she needed the twenty-five cents an hour and the two dollars and fifty cents she earned in tips. However, she had three children at home and needed better hours, so the management, descendants of the Nick Fernandez family, gave her more suitable morning and afternoon hours.

Now eighty-three years old, she works only on Mondays as cashier, and even then, is free to do as she pleases. She is chauffeured to and from work in a private car, per the directive of Robert Maher, one of the owners of Café Du Monde. Retirement will be when she chooses. As I chatted with Mary over cups of café au lait, "Mr. Bob" came over to greet us. Mary asked for permission to give me a couple of Café Du Monde coffee mugs and cans of coffee, to which Robert Maher replied, "Do what you wish." Turning to me, Mary smiled, "He never tells me 'no' to anything." Management even allows Mary to sell her Avon products at the cash register; she is careful to keep her Avon receipts separate from the coffee stand's money.

Reflecting on her forty-five years in the French Market, Mary remembers how her Uncle Sterling Brown would call her from Canal Street before boarding the evening train for Bay St. Louis, Mississippi. The call was for Mary to prepare coffee and beignets for his afternoon repast en route home. Mary filled his order and waited near the track. The engineer slowed the train so that Mary could pass Sterling's order to him as he stood on the back of the last passenger car.

Her magnetic smile attracted customers, especially males. When Mary was much less than eighty-three, a male customer made daily trips to Café Du Monde for his coffee "fix." To get Mary's attention, he always left her a twenty-five-cents tip. As Mary related this story, she interposed with, "In those days, that was a lot of money to me." One morning after a cup of soothing coffee, he said to Mary, "We need to go out sometime. How about it?" She shrewdly delayed giving him a direct answer, for if she said "no" he might not leave the big tip; if she said "yes," her husband and three children would not be too generous in accepting the idea. The days passed and the offers continued. Finally, Mary said, "Okay, I'll go to a movie with you, but you will have to buy five tickets." Her customer-suitor questioned the number of tickets, "Why five?" Mary answered, "One for me, one for my husband, and three for my children." This answer cost Mary her interested customer and his generous tips.

Today, Mary Alexander is as much a part of the Café Du Monde history as the terra-cotta floors, pink walls, green-and-white striped awnings, slowly revolving ceiling fans, and the waiters and waitresses lined along the walls waiting for customers to choose their tables. Another unique feature of the coffee stand, which seats one hundred, is an always-sticky tabletop due to a mixture of water and confectionery sugar. The small, round tables are hastily wiped clean for each new party being seated, for there is always a line of waiting customers. (One of our out-of-town guests, compulsive about nonsticky tables, spent his time cleaning off the table with paper napkins dipped in water from his glass. In spite of how clean he wiped it that night, it was back to its normal tackiness soon after we left.) It all provides a delightful atmosphere for those who want to include the Café Du Monde in their anecdotes about the capital of the Caribbean. To leave Mary out of their stories would be to leave out forty-five years of colorful history.

Carnival Time

There are various rules of order which require certain numbers of participants to have a quorum. What constitutes a quorum for a party in New Orleans? It just takes one person with an umbrella. For social interaction, two people or more is better.

The twelfth night after Christmas is King's Day. Traditionally, it was the time when the wise men visited the Christ child. Significance and times have changed! On this day and until Mardi Gras, circular cakes decorated with green, purple, and yellow granulated sugar are eaten, with everyone hoping to get the slice with the plastic doll hidden in it. Both thrill and obligation come with the excitement of getting the doll—thrill over getting it and obligation to buy the next King Cake.

Carnival, a word derived from the Latin meaning "farewell to the flesh," begins on January 6 and ends on Mardi Gras (French for Fat Tuesday) or Shrove Tuesday (the day before Ash Wednesday, the first day of Lent). The red and green for Christmas are still around when some revelers bring out the purple, green, and gold. It has been a long time since Iberville and Bienville christened the Mardi Gras Bayou, which they discovered on March 3, 1699. Carnival and all its accompaniments have continued to the present, with some modifications and only a few interruptions.

Alvin ("Al") Lee Johnson (he prefers Al) was born to Curtis and Rebecca Johnson in the Flint-Goodridge

Hospital on the tail end of the Great Depression. In his growing-up days in the Lower Ninth Ward, Al played with his chinas (marbles), creating his own games. He would drop a handful of marbles in a hole; the other player contributed the same number of marbles as Al. If an odd number of marbles remained in the hole after being dropped, Al lost. In another game, Al cut holes in cardboard, labelling each hole with a number, for example, four, six, seven, etc. If a contestant shot his chinas through the hole, he won the number of marbles marked above the hole. If he missed, he lost the marble to Al.

Entrepreneurial Al bought a movie projector, charging each viewer a nickel to see the flick. He delivered the *Louisiana Weekly* to residents in the Lower Ninth Ward. He learned to play the trumpet and later shifted to the piano. Talent shows at the Carver, Lincoln, and Caffin Theaters provided Al with five dollars every time he won. As he moved further into his teen years, Al played for the Cadillac Club on St. Claude Avenue, the Top of the Town in Kenner, and the YWCA in the Crescent City. Al Johnson and His Band, with their guitar, drums, saxophone, and piano, were featured here and there at "social and pleasure clubs." All along, his mother insisted that Al finish high school, which he did at Booker T. Washington School.

By 1956 Al had recorded (with the help of Al Matthews) on the Aladdin label, "If I Done Wrong" and "Old Time Talking." When Al was graduated from high school, he began to write and record his own music. His earliest creations were "Lena" and "You Done Me Wrong" on the flip side. As we sat in the Tastee Donuts Shop on Gentilly Boulevard, Al began to sing in subdued tones:

> Hush, Lena, don't cry.
> Don't let our love die.
> I'll love you, Lena,
>
> Roses love sunshine.

Roses love dew.
Lena, my darling.
I'm so in love with you.

You asked me to forgive you
For the wrong you've done.
You asked me to forgive you,
And let you come home.

When I was loving you,
You were doing me wrong.
You were running in the street,
Staying all night long.

Now you want me to forgive you,
And let you come home.
But I could never, never,
Because you done me wrong.

Of course, I was curious to know who Lena was. Al smiled, saying, "She was a girlfriend of my friend. Their relationship inspired me to write it. I got my ideas for lyrics everywhere."

By 1960, Al Johnson had cut another record, "Carnival Time," reflecting his love for and participation in the Carnival season:

The Green room is smoking
And the plaza burning down
Throw my baby out the window
And let those joints burn down
All because it's Carnival Time
Oh Carnival Time
Oh well it's Carnival Time
And every body's [sic] having fun

Claiborne Street is rocking
From one side to the other

On the Stoop

Those joints are jam and pack
And I'm about to smother
All because it's Carnival Time
Oh Carnival Time
Oh well it's Carnival Time
And every body's having fun

Right now it's Carnival Time
Oh Carnival Time
Oh well it's Carnival Time
and every body's having fun

Oh well if you put your nickel
Well now I'll put a dime now
We can get together now and
drink us some wine.
All because it's Carnival Time
Oh Carnival Time
Oh well it's Carnival Time
And every body's drinking wine (© 1979 by Al Johnson)

By Al's own confession he was more "Sunday-school smart" than "street smart." He did not know about copyrights until he realized that his music was more profitable for others than for himself. By 1979 he had "Carnival Time" copyrighted, and soon after got legal rights to his next composition, "Mardi Gras Strut":

Rain, slop, sleet or snow,
This time of year there is a big free show
In New Orleans,
It's a beautiful scene,
Some call it Mardi Gras
Some call it Carnival Time

Uptown, downtown, all around,
It's such a pleasure to be in this town,
They call New Orleans,

98

Carnival Time

It's a beautiful scene,
Some call it Mardi Gras,
Some call it Carnival Time.

Kings, queens and presidents too,
All want a coconut from King Zulu,
In New Orleans,
It's a beautiful scene,
Some call it Mardi Gras.
Some call it Carnival Time.
Bacchus, Endymion and other parade krewes
Throw a lot of doubloons to me and you,
In New Orleans,
It's a beautiful scene
Some call it Mardi Gras
Some call it Carnival Time

(Instrumental musical solo)

All people, rich and poor
All get together for this big free show,
In New Orleans,
It's a beautiful scene.
Some call it Mardi Gras.
Some call it Carnival Time.
Rex and the Mayor meet at Gallier Hall
After they toast they have a Mardi Gras Ball
In New Orleans,
It's a beautiful scene
Some call it Mardi Gras
Some call it Carnival Time
Seafood, Gumbo, red beans and rice
You eat it once
You will have to eat it twice
In New Orleans
It's a beautiful scene
Some call it Mardi Gras
Some call it Carnival Time   (© 1990 by Al Johnson)

On the Stoop

As Al sipped his coffee, I looked into his eyes—saddened by creative losses, mistakes, and exploitation due to his inexperience—and inquired, "What's next, Al?" A twinkle in his eyes brought a faint smile to his face: "I want to write gospel music, and maybe someday Spike Lee will pick up my story for a movie. In the meantime, I'll keep driving White Fleet Taxi No. 715 to pay the bills."

Hunt the Hay

James ("Jim") Cloutman first observed life in 1934 at 2922 Napoleon Avenue. Five years later, Dorothea ("Dottie") Klatt experienced her first awareness of life at 441 Henry Clay Avenue. They would meet for the first time years later on a blind date. As they exchanged stories about their growing-up years in New Orleans, they discovered some similar experiences, such as front-porch gatherings with their friends to discuss what was happening in and around the neighborhood. More often, however, the places they talked about were the same, but their experiences weren't, reflecting mainly the social differences for boys and girls at that time.

Jim's father, James Bradbury Cloutman, worked for the Bell System until he became a victim of the Great Depression. He then worked for his wife's family business, Schenk Realty, maintaining and supervising the family properties. On Sundays, his father's pool buddies came over for a few games and some home brew—the entire first floor of their home was reserved for the pool table. On the second floor were the dining room and formal parlor, where friends gathered on special occasions to hear his mother Ida play the baby grand piano and his father sing. James and Ida sometimes performed at Saint Rose of Lima Church on Bayou Road.

At age fourteen Jim got his first two-wheeled bicycle. Demonstrating the incautious courage of youth, he and his buddies rode to and across the Huey P. Long bridge. In defense of his adolescent judgment, however, it is only fair to mention that this occurred during World War II when there were few automobiles on the road because of gasoline rationing. Less exciting, but also far less dangerous, was the game of stickball that Jim and his friends played with a broomstick and a tennis ball, marking off a vacant neighborhood as their baseball diamond.

Some evenings, Jim enjoyed sneaking off to the French Quarter to hear the music on Bourbon Street, and maybe even catch a glimpse or two of a striptease act. He also liked to slip into night court on North Rampart Street to see the judicial proceedings in progress. He remembers the ritual: the ladies of the evening were the first to appear before the judge; then came the vagrants and the drunks. He remembers one particularly interesting case. The defendant, a man from Iowa, was charged with refusing to pay for the french fries he ordered at a restaurant. The defendant argued that citizens from Iowa did not pay for potatoes. That twenty-five-cent order of french fries cost him a twenty-five-dollar fine.

Dottie was born to Richard and Ella Ernst Klatt. Her maternal grandfather, Karl Ernst, owned and operated the Ernst Hotel on Poydras Street and St. Charles Avenue, where One Shell Square is now located. Richard Klatt was a German immigrant who came to America with his [butcher] "steel and knife" and went to work for Schott and Company. He was conservative and was eventually able to save enough money to buy his own house and market at Henry Clay Avenue and Laurel Street. Although the Klatts lived above the meat market, neither Dottie nor her two brothers were allowed to play in or around it. Richard was such a perfectionist in his trade that one customer jokingly remarked, "If I ever have an operation, I want you to do the cutting because you would never, ever leave a scar."

Dottie received a bicycle when she was eleven years old. She rode only on safe uptown streets, which is what girls were supposed to do. As she matured into adolescence, she was allowed to stay out until midnight one night a week. Her strict German parents informed her dates, "Dorothea will be home at twelve o'clock." She was directed by her parents, "Never go to the French Quarter."

As children, Jim and Dottie both played a game called "hunt the hay." The rules in their separate neighborhoods were the same: participants hid and the person who was "it" had to find them, yelling, "Hunt the hay!" before proceeding.

After they began dating, Jim escorted Dottie to one of their favorite night spots on Airline Drive, Fouray's Southern Tavern. They danced to jukebox music and enjoyed an occasional Coke. On other nights out, they went to the Beaconette at South Claiborne and Napoleon Avenue or Ched's on Milan Street and St. Charles Avenue. They were married in 1954, and have two children, Cherie and Jim III.

Jim invested his time in a sales career with I. L. Lyons and Company, a wholesale pharmaceutical company that stocked thirty thousand items. In 1974 Dottie pursued her interest in nursing and now invests her time at the intensive care unit at East Jefferson Hospital. She makes sure, however, that she finds time for both saltwater and freshwater fishing.

The days of stickball and hunt the hay are far behind Jim and Dottie. After thirty-seven years together, however, life is still in full swing for them.

A Pontchartrain Beach Boy

The title suggests a member of the well-known musical group. It actually describes William ("Curly") Anthony Wagnam, Jr., who for nearly forty years worked as an electrician for Playland Amusement, operator of the Pontchartrain Beach Amusement Park.

Curly was employed for a short time with the Orleans Dredging Company—he says it was only because he could swim. He then went to work as an electrician for the amusement park—at that time called Spanish Fort—located on Bayou St. John near Robert E. Lee Boulevard. He was hired as an electrician, which seemed specialized enough; however, his duties included doing everything there was to be done on the Seaplane, a ride in which passengers "flew" round and round in small airplanes suspended on cables, and the Loop-O-Plane, in which eight or more passengers were securely buckled into each cage-like car and then twirled round and round. His starting salary was $17.00 a week, and it was raised to $17.50 when he informed his boss that he was considering other employment.

By 1939 the amusement park had been relocated to Lake Pontchartrain at Elysian Fields Avenue. Curly was now the head electrician, working on rides called the Wild Cat, Zephyr (roller coaster), Whip, Bug, Roll-O-Plane, Fly-O-Plane, and the Ride & Laugh. Although primarily an electrician, Curly was a jack-of-all-trades. He did whatever Harry Batt and his descendants asked him to do to keep the rides running. If metals needed welding during a weekend (when a welder wasn't available), Curly did the job. Curly drifted off into thought, then returned to the conversation, "Well, at least the rides continued until Monday."

As Curly recalled his days at Pontchartrain Beach, he couldn't avoid remembering some of the accidents that occurred, scenes he described as "near misses to hits." On one occasion he looked up toward the Fly-O-Plane and saw a coat flying through the air. A co-worker remarked, "Look! A coat is flying through the air." They soon realized that someone was *wearing* the coat. Fortunately the flying person landed unharmed in a cedar tree. Another time a squall appeared suddenly, knocking out power and leaving ski lift riders suspended high above the ground. A woman panicked and wanted to toss her children out and then jump herself—it took urgent persuasion to keep her from doing it. The drama continued for at least ninety minutes, but thanks to the New Orleans Fire Department and its extension ladders, it ended without any casualties. The Wild Maus ride didn't escape uninvited excitement either. Curly recalls the time when one of the cars stopped suddenly, causing it to be rammed by the car behind it. The force of the collision propelled a woman out of the car. She landed in a seated position; and although embarrassed, she was not injured. She quickly got up and got lost in the crowd.

There were times, however, when an accident led to tragedy. On a Fourth of July holiday, a rider on the Zephyr tried to move to another car as the train climbed the trestle. He lost his balance and fell to his death.

Curly spent his career surrounded daily by people experiencing the unique fun and excitement found only at an amusement park. His days are much quieter now. At eighty-three years old, the Pontchartrain Beach Boy spends his time carving wood into figures of animals, people, and an assortment of religious symbols.

A Baby in the Rectory

Ordinarily, when the words *rector* and *rectory* are spoken or written, the listener or reader thinks of a clergyman and the place where he lives. When these words are used in a Roman Catholic setting, *rector* and *rectory* suggest celibate priests. In this restricted context, it would appear to be inappropriate, to say the least, and in violation of a canon law, to say the most, for there to be a baby in a Roman Catholic rectory. However puzzling and contradictory, there was a baby named Arissa in the Saint Patrick's Church rectory at 724½ Camp Street.

The story of Arissa began with a caring sexton named Harry Hoey. As a sexton, Harry did not fit the stereotype. After finishing the Sacred Heart School in Hattiesburg, Mississippi, and one year at the University of Southern Mississippi, Harry's life fell under the control of international happenings. From 1941 to 1945 he served in the United States Army. Upon returning from the Big War, Harry thought he would get on with his life. He married Margaret Johnson and studied law at Atlanta Law School for a year and a half. They adopted Susan, and it appeared that smooth, middle-class living lay ahead for them. However, in 1948 he was called back into the United States Army because of the threat of war in Korea. Harry decided to remain in the military service until he could retire in 1964. Not incidental to his future, he received training as a nurse while in the Army, becoming a registered nurse. He and his family returned to

Atlanta; he had been working in the chemical industry for sixteen years when his wife Margaret became terminally ill. During the months of her illness, until her death in 1980, he devoted himself to her care.

After Margaret's death, he chose to move to New Orleans to be among friends and relatives. It was here that he was introduced to the Monsignor of Saint Patrick's Church. The Monsignor asked Harry to assume the responsibilities as sexton because of an extensive renovation project in the church; this eventually required Harry to live in the rectory. During this time, Harry involved himself with Parents Without Partners to give him much-needed emotional balance in his life. He invited the single partners to enjoy the ambiance of Saint Patrick's courtyard and even assumed leadership in the organization, contributing fresh ideas such as the program entitled, "Unconditional Love."

Harry requested the Monsignor to hire an assistant for him. His request was granted and Gary Tebay was hired. Gary needed emotional support because of his interaction with drugs as well as vocational and educational encouragement. Harry gave him the firm encouragement he needed. Gary eventually married and he and his wife had a daughter, which meant more residents in the rectory. Gary's wife also had problems with drugs and chose to walk away from the rectory, leaving newborn Arissa with her husband and Harry. Since Gary was going to school and working, Harry became nurse, mother, and father during most of Arissa's early months. Throughout the hammering and sawing going on during the church's renovation, Arissa was cradled adjacent to the rectory. The workers and subcontractors gave the baby special attention as they passed by.

Bonding was occurring between Harry and Arissa, affectionately referred to by the sexton as "my little buddy," but he knew that more permanent care was needed. Harry sought state and federal help. The state's response was that Arissa's environment was healthier than any they could offer. Federal resources were nonexistent. It appeared that the "little buddy" would remain in the rectory for the unforeseeable future—maybe until she was grown. Who knew?

Harry, however, wanted and sought the best for Arissa. Because of his warm relationship with his own daughter (she had been an adopted baby), Harry turned to Susan. She and her husband took Arissa into their home until Gary's parents in Butler, Pennsylvania, were able to assume responsibility for their granddaughter.

The former baby in the rectory is now living comfortably with her grandparents. Gary has been graduated from school, is gainfully employed, and engaged to be married. In time, Arissa will be reunited with her father. Harry continues to contribute monthly to Arissa's expenses by sending her a check for her own bank account. He makes regular grandfatherly visits to Butler, Pennsylvania, and has the honored status of being a chosen grandparent.

Transporter of Ice and People

Throughout Theodore Graff's adult years, he either transported ice or people. During the 1920s, in his middle to later teens, Ted delivered ice to H. Sophie Newcomb College and Tulane University. He loaded his truck with six to eight 300-pound slabs of ice for these educational sites and unloaded and carried them to the attics to be used for ice water. When he finished his deliveries to the schools, he was off to Carrollton for residential deliveries, twenty-five to one hundred pounds for each customer. Ted feels a flush of embarrassment when he remembers accidentally dropping one hundred pounds of ice on a lady's kitchen floor. It was during the summer in the late 1920s, before air-conditioning systems. The scattered chunks of ice went everywhere, melting into puddles quicker than Ted could retrieve the pieces.

Ted's next employment involved transportation as well, but this time he was transporting people. A conductor was needed for a train operating on one long track at Pontchartrain Beach. Ted was the man, going back and forth, switching at each end of the track. Wanting to remain in transportation, but desiring to advance, Ted, along with Harry Batt, his boss at Pontchartrain Beach, went to New Orleans Public Service, Incorporated (NOPSI) to apply for work. He and three or four others were hired and instructed to report to the Arabella Barn.

With the nation still in the depression in 1932, Ted hired on with NOPSI as a streetcar conductor. The fare for each passenger was seven cents. His duties were as simple as the fares were cheap. Ted collected the fares, issued transfers, and pulled one strap to register transfers and another to record cash fares. The only unpleasant part of his job was ejecting rowdies or undesirables from the streetcar. This part of his job description is one Ted would just as soon forget, but he does recall awakening a sleeping passenger who came to consciousness swinging his fists. Ted had no other choice but to subdue and eject him, which he did.

As streetcars phased out, Ted became a driver of a city bus. He still operated out of the Arabella Barn and transported people up and down Broadway, Laurel, Magazine, and Freret Streets and Claiborne and Jackson Avenues. As a bus driver, his duties were about the same as when he was a streetcar conductor; the basic difference was that he drove instead of conducted. Over the years Ted, the ice-deliverer-turned-people-deliverer, became acquainted with his regular customers as they deposited their seven-cent fares. As we talked, Ted pulled thoughts out of his eighty-year-old brain, paused, and wondered, "I don't know what they charge now. Do you?" I assured him that the price has increased beyond seven cents. The seven-cents fare reminded the transportation man that the biggest raise he ever got from NOPSI was twelve cents per hour.

Mortician by Day — Two-stepper by Night

Some combinations do not mix, such as streetwalking and street preaching. Other activities such as hog calling and opera singing both require strong vocal skills, albeit very different ones. But what about Glen Howard Butler's combination of being a mortician by day and a two-stepper by night? As odd a mixture as it might appear, Glen views burying the dead and keeping time with the music to be complementary.

His work as a mortician began when he chose to drop out of Jones County Junior College in Mississippi. The Sumerall Funeral Home in Laurel, Mississippi, offered him a job and later encouraged him to learn more about the embalming profession by attending the Cincinnati College of Mortuary Science. After learning the skills, Glen returned to the Sumerall Funeral Home. Another job opportunity led him to join the staff of the McBride Funeral Home in Ripley, Mississippi. By 1950 the young mortician had moved to the Crescent City and was working for J. Garic Schoen on Canal Street, where he has remained to the present time, now managing Jacob Schoen and Son, Incorporated.

While he was in Ripley, Glen responded to an ambulance call to transport a patient home from the local hospital. As he prepared for the trip, he asked the nurse standing nearby to hold his overcoat. This was the beginning of a relationship with registered nurse Susie Morton that would lead to their marriage in 1951. After forty years of marriage, Susie now insists that Glen hold his own topcoat.

Since 1955, Glen alone has handled over five hundred funeral arrangements. His caring nature has blended well with Schoen's policy of providing professional and compassionate service to bereaved families. A typical demonstration of this occurred when a New Orleans street performer died. Personal friends were neither available nor able to pay for a burial, so Glen and Schoen agreed to offer free services. More than one hundred sympathizing fellow musicians attended the funeral. On another occasion, Glen read in the *Times-Picayune* about a local woman who had once been wealthy, but who had lost all of her money because of her lavish life-style. With the consent of Garic Schoen, services were arranged without charge.

By day, Glen Butler, wearing an appropriate dark-colored business suit, provides his services for the deceased and their grieving families. Understandably, his evening hours require different clothing and a changed demeanor. Until recently, however, his evening hours were just a boring sameness—eating, reading and sleeping. All of that changed about six years ago when Susie called him at work to inform him that they were going to take Cajun dancing lessons.

Since Susie's directive, most evenings Glen and Susie can be found in either Michaul's Live Cajun Music Restaurant (their favorite place for eating and dancing) or at local churches, where they teach Cajun dancing free of charge to eager, limber learners. Glen and Susie focus on the basic Cajun dancing: the Cajun waltz, two-step, and jitterbug. Favorite Cajun songs for their lessons are "The Backdoor" and "Marksville Two-Step" for the fast-paced dances and "Waltz of Life" and *"Joli Blond"* for the waltz.

Glen has added another dimension to his nightlife.

He learned music in high school, studying the french and bass horns. He has shifted his musical skills to playing Cajun music. He plays the washboard, triangle, and spoons with the Don Duet Cajun Pals and the P. D. Decant Cajun Band for nights of Cajun merriment.

When he was in his mid-fifties, Glen enrolled at Holy Cross College and received his bachelor's degree. He learned Cajun dancing and began playing Cajun musical instruments in his late fifties and early sixties. One could label all of this Glen's mid-life experiences. One thing is certain: he has approached all of these changes and new experiences with zest. Of his new nightlife, he says, "It has changed my life."

The Belly Robber

Nicknames have a way of sticking. Vincent Paul Poret has had more than one; at various times in his adult life he has been called "Belly Robber," "Pop," or "Old Timer."

New Orleans has always been his home. He was born at 8800 Palm Street and now lives just a few blocks from there at 3939 Hamilton Street. As a growing boy, he referred to Rampart Street as the "Ramp," played baseball across from the Union Station, and saw his share of action (violence) on the streets. He remembers four other railroad stations in New Orleans: Texas & Pacific on Annunciation Street, L&N Station at the foot of Canal Street, the Kansas City Southern Station on South Rampart Street, and the Southern Railroad Station on Basin Street. He remembers that he wasn't eligible for free lunch at school because his father made fifty cents an hour doing construction work.

After he was discharged from the Marine Corps following World War II, and until he was recalled to serve in the Korean War, Vincent worked as a baker for the 4th Army at 4400 Dauphine Street. It was here that he picked up his first nickname. The enlisted men referred to him and the other food service employees as the "Belly Robbers." The implications were obvious—those serving Army meals were depriving them (robbing their bellies) of the tasty food they were accustomed to.

After his tour of duty in Korea, Vincent returned

to work for the Army, but the call to drive a taxi was loud and clear. He hired on with Ed's Cab Company and remained with them from 1969 to 1973, when he went to work for the White Fleet Cab Company. As a taxi driver, he acquired new nicknames. His fellow drivers have honored him with "Pop" or "Old Timer." Vincent says his nicknames are certainly superior to names that have tagged some of his other colleagues, such as "Pig" and "Frog." Vincent is still with White Fleet Cab, driving his leased cab a few hours every day, or "as I feel like it."

When he started in the business, cab fares ran fifty cents for the first one-half mile and ten cents for each additional one-fourth mile. The most generous tip he ever received was forty-five dollars. The best of his workweeks will now net him three hundred dollars. Says Vincent, "It ain't the best, but, it ain't bad. It's a hustle."

Driving a taxi has humorous as well as harrowing moments. Once, a lady with her poodle hired his cab to search for her husband. She sat in the rear seat, put the poodle in the front seat next to Vincent, and directed him to drive from bar to bar to locate her errant husband. Another time a passenger hopped in Vincent's cab and paid him ten dollars to take him to the Charity Hospital because he had been shot.

As a precaution, Vincent insists that any passenger carrying a suspicious-looking bag sit on the front seat and keep the bag closed. He had just such a passenger when suddenly a motorcyclist approached and began shooting at the cab. Bullets grazed and penetrated the body of the cab. Vincent decided that his life depended on a speedy escape to the Carrollton Shopping Center, where a police patrolman was usually stationed. Vincent made it safely to the shopping center and got police assistance. He discovered that his passenger and the motorcyclist had been involved in a series of robberies and that his passenger was attempting to double-cross his accomplice by making off with the loot. The suspicious looking bag contained stolen jewelry and money.

His cabby friends also tell interesting stories of their experiences. He recalled his friend Sydney's story of a passenger that approached him: "Are you Sydney?"

"Yes, I am."

"Well, I robbed you of thirty dollars a few years back. Here's your thirty dollars. I've gone to jail and am out. I'm now a minister."

A passenger once asked Vincent what he considers a good day. Vincent responded, "When I pull in and walk in my house in one piece." After he shared this philosophical statement with me, I asked him, "Would he do it all over again?" He responded without a blink, "Yes, I would."

Bag and Baggage

The equestrian life comes naturally to Eric Blind and his family. His father was a horseman and his two sons have continued the tradition. As a four-year-old in Vancouver, British Columbia, Eric was already astride horses; by age fourteen he was a jockey, weighing only ninety-five pounds, and had won his first race in Tijuana, Mexico.

Eric's racing career began when he was offered a contract by David Elander to ride as a jockey after being observed galloping a horse. The contract provided food, clothing, shelter, and some money. Eric began to make his mark as a jockey, however, after Colonel E. R. Bradley bought his contract for five thousand dollars. His career transported him from California to Ohio, Missouri, Louisiana, and Kentucky. He was riding a horse named "Bag and Baggage" when he won the Louisiana Derby and placed in the Kentucky Derby. He had a few more wins and a couple of spills—he injured his jaw when he fell on a fence and hurt his arm the next time he went down—but he decided to "hang it up" three years later at age seventeen. Although he had quit racing horses, he would spend his career working with herbivorous quadrupeds.

Returning to Vancouver, Eric "fooled around with the tracks." Since he was accustomed to being on the move, he chose to go south to San Francisco where he rubbed horses for about five years. My imagination and curiosity flew in different directions. What was "rubbing horses"? Realizing that I did not understand his esoteric language, he explained: *rubbing* meant grooming.

When Eric no longer found the California tracks exciting, he moved from track to track in Michigan, Texas, Illinois, Maryland, and states in-between. In Maryland, he developed expertise in another phase of horse racing: working with his brother Edward, he learned to be a starter. The starter hires six or more assistants to help him handle the horses at the starting gate, keeping them from rearing up, pawing, or flipping over backwards. The assistants manage the horses while the starter mounts the stand to pull the trigger, ringing the bell and opening the stall gates for the race. This is the way it was suppose to happen. Eric confessed his embarrassment when once it did not go as planned. He had tested the gates five times; they worked perfectly. When the time came to start the thirteenth race, Eric pulled the trigger and eleven horses came out. The stall gates failed to open for two horses and their jockeys.

From 1955 to 1985, Eric worked as a starter at the New Orleans Fairgrounds. What does it take to be a starter? Eric was quick to respond with the word, "Honor." It takes good assistants at the gate and fairness with the horsemen (trainees) and jockeys. *Respect* was another one of Eric's key words. A starter has to both respect and be respected by everyone in the business: jockeys, trainers, owners, track superintendents, bookkeepers, racing secretaries, and general manager.

Eric is now eighty-two years old and retired. These days he spends most of his time with his wife Emma, who is ill. His sons Eric and Eddie are starters; he has four grandchildren. In his white, yellow-trimmed house on Colbert Street are pictures of horses, racetracks, and an autographed picture of jockey Chris McCarron. His most recent spill occurred, not on the track, but when he fell and broke his ankle as he was taking out the trash. His eyes twinkled as he said, "I would do it all over again." Although he no longer rides, Eric is a horseman and always will be.

Major Bussey

As Margaret Bussey Willoughby digs around in her eighty-two year-old memory, the earliest recollection she comes up with is a crisis, the death of her mother in 1917. It was the epidemic of influenza which left Margaret and her two brothers with few choices for survival. One which she never regrets having been chosen for her and her brothers was their move to live in the Connie Maxwell Orphanage (Children's Home in Greenwood, South Carolina). Each of the cottages housed four adults and twenty children. This was home for her until she was graduated from high school. When asked for words which describe her years at Connie Maxwell, Margaret lowered her head to reflect. Then she lifted her head and her eyes became fixed in an upward recall position: "Joy, love, appreciation, happiness, chores, duties, and obligations." After these words, she followed with, "I attribute my early life there to forming my character and the way I believe."

Margaret was a person of dreams, which included college and teaching. She accomplished the former at Women's College (Furman University, Greenville, South Carolina), but the latter was never realized. New Orleans altered this dream. She was influenced to come to the Crescent City to study nursing at Baptist Hospital, from which she was graduated in 1935. After a year of specialty study in surgery at Stanford University, Margaret returned to the port city to serve as supervisor of the operating room at Baptist Hospital on Napoleon Avenue.

Another crisis influenced Margaret in 1942. World War II affected not only her, but all other people of the globe. Deployed from New Orleans were two military hospitals formed to serve the troops: the 24th and 64th General Hospitals, which followed the fighting from Africa to Italy. Margaret joined the Army Nurse Corps and was assigned to the 64th. By the time she returned to New Orleans, she had been promoted to the rank of captain; she was mustered out of the Corps as a major. As she withdrew reflecting on her stint in the Big War, her words expressed her feelings: "Need, service, fear, apprehension, and sympathy."

Before she went overseas with the hospital unit, a friendship began between Margaret and Dr. Robert Madison Willoughby, a urologist who would also be assigned to the 64th General Hospital. Their friendship continued throughout the war and by 1953 they were married, remaining together until his death in 1966. Margaret characterized this period of her life as "giving and sharing."

Since Robert's death, Major Bussey has devoted her life to serving others through her beloved First Baptist Church on St. Charles Avenue. If she is not giving her time to young adults, she is sharing herself with older adults. On a regular weekly basis, Margaret, along with her friend Betty Breen, invites persons who have not yet been integrated into New Orleans life for a Sunday lunch. Each Sunday, as many as twenty-four people are invited to be their guests. Included among the guests are medical and theological students as well as a variety of other persons who need and want special caring treatment. For a recent Christmas, Margaret and Betty invited as many as sixty people to a festive meal. Major Bussey receives and chooses to search out people who need encouragement and someone to talk to. Reflecting on her eighty-two years, Margaret states, "I would take the same route and make the same decisions. I have no regrets."

Poppa Joe

In the French Market, stalls 1—11 on the lake side and 2—12 on the river side are leased by partners Joe Mustachia and Freddie Dolice. Freddie, incapacitated by a stroke, is no longer able to work at the market. However "Poppa Joe," as Joe is affectionately called, continues to handle the sale of Louisiana hot peppers, delicious apples, sweet satsumas, Chiquita bananas, strings of chili peppers, and white Creole garlic. On any given day Poppa Joe, who stands five feet seven inches tall and weighs just over two hundred pounds, will be casually dressed in a plaid shirt, an English cap covering most of his forehead, and a pair of wide black suspenders holding up his trousers.

Poppa Joe is a quiet man. Early each morning he may be found either checking his competitors' prices or those of the wholesalers on the river side of French Market Place. Throughout the day, he will be either in his cluttered, eight-by-twelve-foot office tending to the management end of his business, or among his boxes of produce making sales to the tourists who want snacks such as three sweet satsumas or a bag of Cajun Creole hot peanuts. Poppa Joe is assisted during the day by Arthur, formerly in the finance business, who donates his time to Joe, and to Joe Mustachia, Jr., who keeps his father's "doorless and windowless" business open twenty-four hours a day.

To the best of Poppa Joe's seventy-two-year-old

memory, he and Freddie began their produce business in the 1940s. He remembers that their sales then were exclusively on the river side of North Peters Street. New Orleans customers would line up in their automobiles along the curb, placing their produce orders and getting instant delivery without leaving their vehicles. Decades ago, customers never handled the produce—touching, squeezing, smelling, or tasting—the way they do today. The broad walkway through the center of the French Market now allows customers to pick and choose what they wish.

Looking back just to the 1940s is not far enough to reach Poppa Joe's business roots. As a boy in the 1920s and 1930s, young Joe sold apples and oranges from house to house uptown, pulling his wheelbarrow with a strap tied around his neck. Like a town crier, he called out, "Apples and oranges!" Later he used a horse and wagon to deliver different products, coal and wood. His territory consisted of the streets between Napoleon Avenue and Audubon Park.

When he married Josephine fifty-two years ago, Poppa Joe, along with his partner Freddie, began their venture in the French Market. At age twenty and married, young Joe focused on produce sales, remembering what his father had taught him:

Always be honest.

Don't take a nickel that doesn't belong to you.

These early moral lessons taught him never to sell a customer bruised or damaged fruit and vegetables. As we talked, he reached into a large, clear glass gallon jar full of nickels. Fingering the coins, he reflected proudly, "Freddie and I never took one of these from each other."

At age seventy-two, Poppa Joe observes that his customers are no longer just native New Orleanians, but mainly tourists from everywhere; that prices have soared from a few pennies for an apple to three for a dollar; and that the markup is minimal. Still he intends to remain at Ursulines Avenue and North Peters Street, even though he could collect social security and retire. He remembers that his friend Charlie collected his first social security check and died. The French Market is his business home and it is here that he intends to remain and live.

Behind the Charlie Horse

You can easily locate the Fuhrmann residence on Oaklawn Street in Old Metairie even if you don't know the address. Just look for the handmade wooden horse head which is anchored on a post between the *banquette* (a New Orleans sidewalk) and the curb. Emile Fuhrmann affectionately refers to this horse as the "Charlie Horse." At Christmastime Charlie is decorated with red and green; for Easter he wears a fancy hat; and, you guessed it, Charlie is draped in purple, green, and gold during the Mardi Gras season. No. 4 Oaklawn Street has been Emile and Caroline Fuhrmann's home since 1942. It is where they reared their children, Susie and Wayne, and where Emile has periodically practiced architecture and civil engineering (his office has sometimes been in his home and at other times in New Orleans) since receiving Architect License No. 47 from the State of Louisiana.

Emile Fuhrmann has lived a full, productive life since his birth in 1911 in Goodbee, Louisiana. He was graduated from Tulane University, licensed to practice architecture, served in the military, practiced his profession alone and with others, and is qualified to be a member of Mensa (an organization of persons who rank in the top 20 percent of the thinking people in the world) and Intertel (the 1 percent elite of Mensa). Emile's architectural designs include the Saint John United Church of

Christ and the Episcopal Church of the Holy Comforter, both in New Orleans, and the Metairie Evangelical and Reformed Church.

When he designed the Metairie Evangelical Church in 1949, Emile focused on his interests in wood and wood carving. His design included carved religious symbols on the pulpit and above the altar. The contractor, however, was unable to locate someone to do what Emile required. Exasperated, he turned to Emile for help, requesting that *he* carve the cross on the pulpit and the dove above the altar. This marked the official beginning of Emile's avocation as a wood-carver. Emile was later asked to carve bas-reliefs for the nave of the church. For decades worshipers have admired his carved symbols of the Christian Church: a ship, an ark, a vine, seven candlesticks, a rock, and wheat and tare.

Emile's interest in working with wood developed long before he began designing churches. His mother, recognizing both his creativity and his need for something to occupy his time, gave fourteen-year-old Emile one of the posts from a massive four-poster bed so he could make whatever he chose. The result was a writing desk. Living in rural Goodbee gave Emile the opportunity to be creative; making things with his hands became a large part of his fun. He made blocks from the yellow clay and toys from tin cans. Emile probably inherited his woodworking talent from his mother's Bavarian father, Robert Hilgner, who was a master craftsman. Prominently displayed in the Fuhrman home, and proudly pointed out by Emile, are pieces of furniture designed and crafted by Grandfather Hilgner: a walnut sleigh bed, a mahogany sideboard, and an armoire with decorative carvings of leaves and vines.

Emile's woodwork begins in his cluttered, but organized, shop in the rear of his home. The shop houses his band saw, drill, handsaws, and screwdrivers. The surface of his workbench reflects the patina of age and use. Of all his tools, Emile maintains that his claw hammer and handsaw are his basic tools. His inside workroom (daughter Susie's former bedroom) is where he does his intricate wood carving and keeps his carving stool, a vice to hold a block of wood (his favorite woods are mahogany, pine, and poplar), and his chisels, many of which he made himself.

Emile's finished art objects are everywhere in his home. In addition to being beautifully crafted, many of the pieces have an obvious utilitarian purpose. He made a cane with a curve below the handle, allowing for the weight of his body to be on axis with the shank of the cane. The knob on the grip of the cane is carved to fit comfortably in the hand. A clotheshorse, designed with a carved horse head and three pegs for hanging clothes, stands alongside Emile and Carrie's bed. (This is the bed that he made from Philippine mahogany because "I did not like the bed we had.") When Carrie suffered backaches, he invented a pick-up stick with a trigger in the handle which controlled tweezers to pick up objects, even as small as a safety pin. Nearby stands a cypress desk with a drop lid front. With a grin, Emile confessed that he made the desk "to keep Carrie out of my things."

Emile's wood carvings are created solely for artistic expression. One depicts two scenes of a cowboy, before and after a roundup. Before the event, the cowboy and his horse are alert and exuberant with anticipation; after the roundup, the cowboy's shoulders droop and the horse's head hangs in exhaustion. In the living room hang bas-reliefs of Adam and Eve; the Spanish Main; and the Defender of Troy, Hector and his wife Andromache. Carrie prefers that he not display a couple of his carvings, two Africans in the nude, but Emile insists that the works remain in full view. A carving titled "Hurricane" was inspired by the 1969 Hurricane Camille. Waves in the background depict force; and a fierce, four-toothed head with a clenched fist beneath it symbolizes the massive destructiveness of a Gulf Coast hurricane.

Architecture and civil engineering have been

Emile's mainstay, but his woodwork has given him and many others years of pleasure. Look for the Charlie Horse. He is only a small example of the treasures that have been created in the modest house at No. 4 Oaklawn Street.

Cames and Joints

Cames and *joints* may not be significant terms to most people, but to A. Henry Lips the two words constitute a daily part of his artistic work. Day after day he and his son Albert solder slender, grooved bars of lead to hold pieces of stained glass together. When they notch and bend the cames together and solder the joints to complete their original design or to repair a previously designed window, they have finished products like the stained-glass windows which can be seen at Saint John the Baptist Church on Dryades Street or the Jackson Avenue Evangelical Congregation Church.

The name Lips and glass have been virtually synonymous for more than 150 years. Along with Henry and his son Albert are Henry's brothers Claude, Julius, and Leon, who are connected with the glass business in one way or another. Henry's father, grandfather, and great-grandfather have all been glass artists. With pride, Henry displayed a stained glass window, created in 1854, and removed from his grandfather's former Chestnut Street residence.

The secrets of stained-glass artistry have been passed from father to son in the Lips family. Each son learns only from his father how to mix paint for stained glass; mix cement, a waterproofing compound; coordinate colors; and to do it all correctly. Each generation of the

Lipses has its personal secrets. Henry has his own instructions for son Albert:

Do it my way or don't do it at all.

My way is the tried and proven way.

If done my way, I'll be responsible for it.

If done your way, you are responsible.

Do it right.

Be honest. Stay with original price; eat your losses.

Young Henry Lips was only seven years old when he began to learn the trade. As his workshops moved from Hope Street to Harmony Street and then to Laurel Street, it was natural for him to bring son Albert into the business at age seven also. Albert hopes to pass on the Lips's tradition, encouraging his young daughters, Kelly and Katie, "to learn glass."

Although born and reared in Orleans Parish, about fifteen years ago Henry chose a new site for his workshop, a 40' X 100' warehouse in Chalmette. The work area has the expected tools and apparatus which any glass artist would have, including a small lead knife with a circular lead head on one end and a hooked knife on the other and a light box which provides the Lipses a visual view of the stained glass. The small office area is cluttered with three desks, a safe, water cooler, small refrigerator, and an assortment of papers, calendars, pieces of rope, and glass tools. When customers call on the telephone requesting a bid or a job completion date, they hear a more patient voice if Albert answers, and a less patient one if Henry responds.

Before the Lips's team re-leads a stained-glass window, they photograph it and also make a lead rub impression of it on kraft paper. Then they remove the window, panel by panel, building a box around the area if necessary to prevent the window from collapsing. An apron covered with a drop cloth is built at the bottom of the box to catch falling pieces of lead or glass. The stained glass is removed and transported to the Lips's work area where the artists do their restoration.

If Henry and Albert are erecting a stained-glass door or window, they will *cartoon* the design. Although they have the expertise to paint and fire the glass, they now rely on other tradesmen like the Grand Rapids Art Glass Company to do this for them. Once they have the glass, they proceed to lead the glass according to their artistic design.

The Lipses work with other types of glass besides stained glass. Their skills also include beveling glass and installing plate glass or float glass. Of course, the general glazing, cutting, and installation of float glass in store fronts is not as artistically demanding as etch beveling and stained glass designing. The beveling process is more complicated and begins with quarter-inch glass and proceeds from wheel to stone until the glass is finally polished. Beveled glass is too heavy for lead, so zinc plated with copper is used to hold the glass in its designed place.

Henry admits that some people say that he is arrogant or that he takes too long to complete a contract. He is straightforward about expressing his opinion that he and Albert know their trade and refuse to do anything less than their best. The beauty of their work confirms what he says. When a design is completed, the customer can expect to enjoy it for a lifetime.

The Encyclopedia Man

Seventy-two-year-old Kenneth Quentin Berger sat across from me on a Henredon sofa at the Hurwitz-Mintz Furniture Company on Royal Street. His graying hair complimented his blue eyes, encircled with bronze-rimmed glasses. It is obvious that the years have not affected his memory—it remains sensitively active. In fact, one of his younger sales colleagues politely requested permission to interrupt our conversation to ask Mr. Berger, his executive sales manager, a question. As the dean of French Quarter salesmen arose and walked toward his inquiring associate, the young man commented, "Kenneth Berger is our encyclopedia."

His father's ancestors, the Bergers, came to the United States from Austria before 1850. His mother's family, the Moraises, came here from Portugal a decade or so earlier. Generations of Bergers and Moraises have maintained their Jewish faith and have upheld their Hebraic traditions, whether Orthodox, Conservative, or Reform. Kenneth and his wife, the former Betty Myer, have passed on to their two daughters the Shema, along with the festival of Passover.

The French Quarter is where Kenneth Berger has always worked. At age seventeen he got his first job with the Waldhorn Company, originally a pawn shop, and now the oldest antique shop on Royal Street. His grandfather, Sidney Elias Morais, had gone to work for the Waldhorn Company in 1881, the year it opened. By

Kenneth's own admission, Tulane University was not his cup of tea—he belonged in retail sales.

Kenneth got his basic sales education at Waldhorn's, then left for "graduate school," working for his uncle at Mervin G. Morais Antiques. He has been working for Hurwitz-Mintz since Valentine's Day, 1966. As he approached age seventy he decided to retire, but Ellis Mintz persuaded him to remain as an interior consultant and executive sales manager. In this capacity, he now serves as the firm's encyclopedia. Ask Kenneth Berger about:

Antiques: The antique business is really a hobby. Dealers "fall in love" with their antiques. When they sell an item, they seek to replace it with another purchase. They are like stamp collectors. Dealers tend to get trapped in their businesses, having to sustain a loss if they choose to get out of the business quickly.

Salesmanship: Practices of salesmanship have changed. Ladies used to come to Royal Street wearing hats and gloves. This was a "royal" event. Sales personnel never rushed a customer. She knew what she had in mind, and the salesman patiently waited for her decision. Advertizing was more word of mouth.

Jewish People: Jewish people tend to live by their wits as opposed to their hands. Because of persecution, they were forced to move from locality to locality. They had to take their "wit-trades" with them. My father worked briefly for the Cumberland Telephone Company, but he was advised to go into business for himself because he was "too pushy." Jewish people who are not self-employed prefer to work for other Jewish people where their style of salesmanship tends not to be resented.

Customers: The ratio of local-customer trade to

tourist trade for Hurwitz-Mintz is 80/20 percent. For antique shops, the ratio is reversed. Customers interested in antiques do not have preconceived notions about furniture—they come to discover. Prospective buyers for currently manufactured furniture have particular pieces in mind. They come to buy. They buy, and they leave. Tourists who enter Hurwitz-Mintz come to browse. They want information in order to buy back home or through a 1-800 catalogue. Years ago customers were personally known, making credit checks unnecessary. G. G. O'Brian came from Chicago to purchase Georgian silver. One man came to New Orleans to buy guns—his wife bought Christmas presents, spending as much as fifty thousand dollars. A female customer came annually from Oklahoma to buy jewelry for her daughters. More often than not, she had to wait eight months to pay—waiting for the crop to come in and be sold. Another customer exclaimed over the amount of Georgian silver coming from the state of Georgia, "I did not realize that they made so much silver in Georgia."

Today there is a correlation between sales contacts and sales. As the contacts increase, the sales increase. Therefore, salesmen cannot spend time just giving information or exchanging stories. However, it is important for a salesman to establish rapport with his customers. This will increase the customers' trust. Because of trust, I am selling to third-generation families.

Furniture: American furniture manufacturers turned away from Mediterranean furniture after the 1976 United States Bicentennial, and toward Eighteenth Century English furniture. Oriental furniture mixes well with modern and traditional pieces. The most popular fine wood is mahogany, being introduced by Thomas Chippendale in the middle of the 1700s. Oak furniture is more informal and was used strongly during the Victorian period. Walnut is more expensive and is used sparingly by manufacturers. Those who know furniture know Baker, Widdicomb, Kindel, Heritage, and Henredon.

Miscellaneous Subjects:

Waldhorn Company is the oldest antique shop on Royal Street.

Selling furniture on commission is like being in business for oneself.

I make money in the furniture business and invest it in stocks and bonds. *

Henry Stein, approaching one hundred years, is the oldest antique dealer in New Orleans.

Small businesses tend to be on the river side of the street. There is more foot traffic on the lake side of Royal. The reason for this phenomenon is the shade on the lake side.

From noon to 4:00 P.M., furniture businesses will make three-fourths of their sales.

When I worked for the Waldhorn Company, I was tipped fifty cents for showing a customer the company's sales items.

Since Hurwitz-Mintz is across from the Monteleone Hotel, I once had a wearied customer to enter the furniture store thinking it was the hotel. The customer ordered me to have someone get his bags out of his automobile parked on Royal Street.

On any day but Monday, the encyclopedia man

will be quietly and discreetly offering information to fellow sales people and customers alike. He and Hurwitz-Mintz have an understanding that whenever he chooses to go to Houston for a family visit or to Belgium or Israel for a pleasure visit, his absence will be explained as "he's out to lunch."

Made No Waves

Isaac Morais, born in 1900, summarizes his life by saying, "I made no waves." Isaac, the only child of Jewish parents, means simply that he was a quiet, retiring kind of person who did not create problems at home, at school—avoiding Principal Hannah White at McDonogh No. 7 who was described as "hell on wheels"—or in his professional career as a certified public accountant (in the days when he says "a dollar was a dollar and a man was a man").

Isaac remembered his parents. He said he resembled his father Eugene. Florentine, his outgoing mother, actively engaged people through her door-to-door salesmanship, selling everything from pecans for a local dealer to hatpin protectors. His mother's home remedy for a cough was sliced and crushed onions with sugar. If that didn't cure him, he was given Brown's Mixture, a patented medicine which promised to cure virtually any malady.

Isaac's family observed the rituals and traditions of their Jewish faith. At Passover the family had matzo crackers, along with a roasted bone and a boiled egg. Uncle Isidore Morais read Hebrew prayers and scriptures. Isaac remembers giggling whenever Uncle Isidore read about the plague of lice. He's not sure why he thought it was so funny, but he was certain of Uncle Isidore's displeasure with his levity. Rabbi Leucht, whom Isaac referred to as a "son of a gun," always scolded the congregation for not coming to the synagogue regularly. Grandmother Simah Morais blessed Isaac and the other children as the need arose.

One of his earliest memories is of standing outside the Frank T. Howard Elementary School No. 2, dreading going inside. His parents moved often because of financial problems, so he also had to transfer to different schools. After Frank T. Howard he transferred to McDonogh No. 7 and then to Live Oak School in Uptown. He attended Warren Easton High School, where he studied only business courses. He admits "he didn't learn much" there. It was enough, however, to direct him toward evening classes at Loyola University, which prepared him to pass his CPA examination.

Recalling his New Orleans neighborhoods, Isaac said that grocery stores dotted every corner; the proprietors gave the children cookies as lagniappe with the purchase of a few items. Beans and rice were staples and could be purchased for half a nickel, a minted coin with a hole in the center. The Bacher Bros. Bakery on or near Laurel Street sold their bread products without wrappers. The Ninth Street Meat Market displayed sirloin steaks openly on a skewer and sold them for thirty-five cents; seven-bone steaks were fifteen cents for two cuts. Kreher's Bakery on Magazine Street sold hot loaf bread for four cents.

As a developing boy, Isaac played under the streetlights on Antonine Street. At that time New Orleans residents deposited their collected trash in wooden boxes. Isaac and his friends determined that the boxes were the perfect fuel for their New Year's Eve bonfire; the next day, the neighbors discovered that quite a few trash receptacles were missing. Otherwise, Isaac and the neighborhood boys were not destructive. Their energies were mostly spent playing outdoor games. A favorite was marbles. Chinas (marbles) were placed inside a circle drawn in the dirt, and were shot at with tars (agatoid shooters). Plumping, a favorite maneuver among the sharpshooters, meant shooting a marble into the air so it would land in the middle of the ring. In the game called stickup, each player threw a stick into the ground, attempting to knock down those thrown by the other players. Mumblety-peg was similar, but played with pocket knives. Each player demonstrated his dexterity by throwing his knife from different positions so that the blade would stick into the ground or a wooden surface

Isaac's memories moved to his working years. He washed and filled catsup bottles at Zatarain's, but his favorite job there was filling small, flat bottles with vanilla extract, pouring the liquid through a narrow rubber tube. The extract was made by soaking vanilla beans in water. He recalled another job, working in the office of a furniture store that employed door-to-door salesmen to sell religious pictures on the installment plan. After making the sale, the salesmen would return weekly to the customer to collect the payments, which were just a few pennies each. It was Isaac's job to record the weekly collections. He also held a stenographer's job with a plumbing business, J. V. Stiefvater, Inc.

As Isaac progressed in his accounting studies, he advanced with each job move. He was hired as an accountant with Derbes, Caballero, and Miller Accountants, and later with J. K. Byrne and Company, where he remained for forty years. Isaac recalls with pride that through his management the New Orleans Wholesale Florists and Supply Company avoided bankruptcy, a fact which gave him great satisfaction.

Today Isaac is a widower who lives alone in the Metairie residence where he and his wife, the former Gladys Robbert, reared their son David and lived for more than fifty years. In devotion to Gladys, Isaac attends her church, the Metairie Evangelical Church, as often as his health allows. He has turned in his CPA certificate because he no longer practices accounting. His New Orleans memories, however, are carefully saved, always ready to be shared.

Viva the Holtrys!

The Holtry roots go deeper than 1893, but this was the year James Addison Holtry was born. The pressure of economics and the apparent futility of getting an education caused James Addison to drop out of school to make money as a self-employed bootblack. Young Holtry shined shoes for seventeen years; but, one of his customers, R. L. Johnson, predicted a much different future for him. The two teamed together, eventually leading to James Addison Holtry becoming president and general manager of the Good Citizens Insurance Company, Good Citizens Funeral System, Good Citizens Drugs, Inc., and Good Citizens Realty Corporation.

Businessman Holtry was not one to hoard his earnings; on the contrary, he shared his money and much more. The broad-shouldered, thick-jowled philanthropist and philosopher developed and shared his philosophy for life:

People are basically good even though they are inclined to look out for themselves first.

The little man will help more than the big man.

Poverty has a way of making us all good.

Make sure when you climb the ladder that you treat
people kindly going up because these are the people
you will meet coming down.

Remember you don't know everything.   Surround
yourself with people who do.

Help yourself; don't look to the "man."

Trust God, if you are right, but be sure you are right.

Maxine Holtry Daniels, the only surviving child of
James Addison Holtry and Ellen Whittington, is among
the persons who benefitted most from her father's influence and generosity. To Maxine, her father was a special
person who did special things with and for her, like taking her to hear Louis Armstrong, Cab Calloway, or Fats
Waller at the Bull's Club across the street from their
home on the corner of Eighth and Danneel Streets.
When her father was not available to escort her to the
club, she sat on the stoop of the family's shotgun house
to hear these and other famous musicians play—they often
played outside the Bulls' Club.

From her uptown residence, she heard the hawking of the watermelon vendors and watched the chimney
sweeps, wearing their traditional garb, go from house to
house. She attended Barnes Preschool, McCarty Elementary School, and was graduated from Gilbert Academy.

As a child, Maxine had both black and white play-
mates, so the color of her skin or that of the other children was immaterial. Her backdoor neighbor was a New
Orleans police officer, whose children she played with
daily. At age five or six she was invited to a party which
was prejudicially blocked by some parents. Only then did
she realized that she was considered different by some.
This was further emphasized during an experience in the
1930s when she boarded a St. Charles Avenue streetcar
after classes at Gilbert Academy.   When the conductor

insisted that she and other blacks sit in the "colored" seating section of the streetcar, they refused. He then moved
the "screen" (a wooden sign fitted to the back of a seat to
specify segregated seating) to where they were sitting, for
he wanted them to know "their place."

Maxine's interest in the arts led to a four-year
study program at the Cincinnati Art Academy where she
majored in sculpting. She then enrolled at Southern University in New Orleans, from which she received her
Bachelor of Arts Degree. She later returned to Cincinnati
to study ceramics for two years with artist Carl Nash.
She pushed for the introduction of a course of study in
mortuary science at Delgado Community College; she and
her husband were the first to receive Associate Degrees in
the field.

The attitude of her father, James Addison Holtry,
was passed on to his daughter Maxine. She taught art
until 1973, first at Gilbert Academy and later for the Orleans Parish School Board. She married Pastor Lawler P.
Daniels, Jr., and devoted another part of her service energy to the Good Faith Pleasant Grove Baptist Church. For
a period of time, Maxine carried the family business ban-
ners; since selling her interests in the family businesses,
she has applied her own entrepreneurial skills in other
directions.

Maxine taught and influenced artist Marguerite
Cassanave Thompson, Atlanta Mayor Andrew Young,
and Judges Robert and Lynell Collins; served with her
husband as king and queen of the Zulu Social and Pleasure Club; and now serves as the Public Relations Director for the Civil Sheriff of Orleans Parish. These accomplishments have not caused her to turn her eyes away
from the needs of street people or her energies from the
needs of young musicians and athletes. Maxine Holtry
Daniels, the daughter of a former bootblack, wants to
help blacks to help themselves and never to forget their
heritage of struggle.

Cab No. 167

You won't find White Fleet Cab No. 167 at busy taxi locations like the New Orleans International Airport or the French Quarter. Seventy-nine-year-old Samuel Tate chooses to work only in the city, specifically, stationed around hospitals and responding to radio calls. When a call comes from the dispatcher, only the first two digits of the addresses are given. The driver responding to the call gives his expected time of arrival (ETA). If Samuel is more than seven minutes away from the pick-up address, he refuses to respond.

Samuel was a originally a construction worker; but when he shattered his knee in an automobile accident, he was forced into less strenuous and physically demanding work. This eventually led him to drive for Elk's Cab Company, where he stayed for nineteen years. He has worked for White Fleet Cabs for eighteen years. Their rules are simple: wear a white cab cap; don't wear sandals, shorts, or a tank top; and keep yourself clean.

As a cab driver, Samuel Tate has been exposed to the good and the bad—he remembers the bad more clearly. Back in the days when sixty cents was enough to see all of New Orleans in a cab, a woman waved him down and asked him to take her from one location to another as she tried to locate her boyfriend. She finally decided to terminate the search when her fare reached seven dollars. She turned to Samuel in bewilderment; she did not have a penny to her name. Her plan had been to find her boyfriend and to get the fare from him. Samuel thought about calling the police, then dismissed the idea. As he was considering other alternatives, the passenger decided to offer her female services to him as payment, suggesting a nearby hotel. Samuel declined her bartering scheme and instead gave her his cab number, "Call me when you get the money." He never heard from her.

Samuel once responded to the dispatcher's call requesting a cab at First and Magnolia Streets. As he slowly cruised by to locate his passengers, he noticed two suspicious looking characters standing in the shadow alongside a building. "Do I stop? Do I not stop?" He went inside to inquire if someone had called; there had been no call. He decided to take a chance on the two since they wanted a cab to take them only a few blocks to Magnolia and Valence Streets. His only pay for his services was a gun barrel pressed against his neck and a demand for his money. That call cost him his day's wages of forty-six dollars and very nearly cost him his life.

Threats come from people of all sizes. A youngster called for a cab to take him to his grandmother's. He didn't know her address, but knew her house when he saw it, so he directed Samuel to Louisiana Avenue. They cruised slowly until he said, "That's it." He asked Samuel to give him change for a twenty-dollar bill for his grandmother; Samuel insisted that his young passenger produce the currency before he handed over the four five-dollar bills. As the exchange took place, the boy grabbed for the bills gripped tightly in Samuel's hand. The tops of the bills were torn off, but fortunately Samuel held onto the larger parts, allowing for full credit at the bank.

Samuel responded to a call made by a woman who was moving out of her apartment. She wanted him to come in and carry out her belongings. He declined and was absolutely convinced that it would have been a bad idea when he saw a seven-foot man standing in the doorway, glaring in his direction with bloodshot eyes.

On another call Samuel discovered a desperate

woman whose clothes had been cut into pieces with a knife. Recognizing that this was a police matter, he called for help. When an officer arrived and surveyed the situation, he counseled, "Lady, both of you admit that he [her boyfriend] bought your clothes. Therefore, he's got the right to do with his property [the clothes] what he pleases."

Samuel retrieved thought after thought, dating all the way back to the middle teens of this century. He recalled his father making twenty-five dollars a week as a semiskilled laborer, when the average black male made only nine. Rent cost his parents eight dollars a month for a fourplex. During the 1930s, as a young man in his early twenties, he could go to the grocery store and pay a nickel for either two loaves of stale bread, a quart of buttermilk, or two thick pork chops; for a dime he could get a link of smoked sausage large enough to serve three people. Rent for him and his wife was seventy-five cents a week. This included only a community bath, so they chose to bathe in their own oval galvanized tub.

Hard work and conservative spending have allowed Samuel Tate to buy his own home and to accumulate enough resources to work leisurely as a cabby. What about his future? He wants a brick house to replace his existing frame home on South Gayoso Street. Upon reaching this goal, he intends to enjoy the beauty and security of his brick house until "it is time to go."

Hot Strings

Hot potato, hot shot, hot pink, hot dog, hot pants, hot wheels, hot sauce, hot sausage, hot weather, hot pepper, hot times, hot story, hot strings. Hot *strings?*

The first twelve *hots* are familiar; the last needs some clarification. Hot Strings simply defines the great New Orleans musical sound coming from the picks, fingers, and bows of violinist Ed Wadsworth, guitarist Hank Mackie, guitarpist Phil DeGruy (he plays his unique seventeen-string guitar), and bassist Eric Glaser. This sophisticated string-swing group plays with a mod French flavor featuring the best from George Gershwin, Cole Porter, Jerome Kern and others. Hot Strings has revived the style of music which was popular in New Orleans in the 1920s and 1930s.

Even though these four make up the Hot Strings, it was Edward Wadsworth, a former federal clerk-of-court professional, who decided to turn from the practice of law to music, eventually organizing the musical group. While seated across from me at a table in Mom's Cafe on Old Metairie Road, Ed unraveled his seventy-two-year-old story. With shoulders slightly stooped and eyes occasionally peering over his gray-rimmed spectacles, Ed sipped his black coffee, pensively considering every word. His words, phrases and sentences were carefully constructed, but his paragraphs often skipped among memories from

148

the 1920s to the 1990s. When he finished, however, his story was complete.

Ed's life began on the day before Independence Day in 1919. His mother Edna Huddleston Wadsworth loved, practiced, and taught piano. His father Edward White Wadsworth was devoted to and practiced law. As a boy growing up in Montgomery, Alabama, he enjoyed his sandlot football, but was persuaded by his music-loving mother to study the piano and then the violin. Along the way, Ed got more pleasure than money playing in a cocktail lounge at the Whitley Hotel (Montgomery), the Ansley Hotel (Atlanta), with the Auburn Knights Orchestra (Auburn University), and with the Alabama Cavaliers (Tuscaloosa). His devotion to music led him to diversify his instruments and skills to include the trumpet and to focus his interest on jazz and the sounds of the Big Band era. By his own admission, however, he had a better "lip" for the violin than for the trumpet.

Uncle Sam had naval plans for him in the early 1940s. By the end of that decade, Ed had been discharged from the Navy, had returned to law school, married Bonnie Murphee, been graduated from the University of Alabama Law School, practiced law in Montgomery, and had been appointed as secretary and law clerk to United States Circuit Judge Leon McCord of the old Fifth Circuit Court of Appeals. Ed's third decade of life had one momentous event after another, including the births of sons Edward M. and Stephen. By the end of his next decade, Ed had been appointed clerk of the entire Fifth Circuit and had moved to New Orleans.

Down deep in Ed Wadsworth was a love for music that never left him. To Ed, the Crescent City was more than a composite of ethnic and national groups and more than just a mass of land mooned by the Father of Rivers—it was the home of jazz. When Ed the lawyer became exposed to the New Orleans sound, his deep love for notes, scores, and the violin resurfaced. In 1979, at the age of sixty, Ed retired from federal service, deciding to devote the rest of his life to Lucia Cuccia, his present wife, and his music.

With the security of his federal pension, Ed set out to reach his musical goals. With a "ton of jazz violin records," his ears listened and his hands, arms, and chin got daily jazz workouts. The next move for the lawyer-turned-musician was to recruit a group of equally enthusiastic string players. When he located Hank Mackie, Phil DeGruy, and Eric Glaser, Hot Strings was born. Development rapidly followed the birth of the group. The ensemble has played its mellow, but swinging sounds, for Jazz and Heritage Festivals, Autumn in Armstrong Park, the Contemporary Arts Center, and for activities on Bastille Day.

Being the "senior partner" in this "music firm", Ed smiled as he reflected humorously on the way the other members pick on him as often as they do their instruments. Commenting on Ed's talent, his colleagues said that he is "one of the best violinists in the country; but in the city, he does not play that good." At the New Orleans Jazz and Heritage Festival in 1991, Ed reported to the group that he had received "a tremendous" number of requests. The group quipped, "Just ignore them and play anyway."

Edward White Wadsworth has always been on the move. Now, at seventy-two, after a career that took him from private law practice to the federal judicial system and from Montgomery to New Orleans, Ed is where he wants to be, devoted to his "jazz fiddle."

Never Again

It goes without saying that some negatives destroy hope. At other times they generate it. The dedication of the Hilda Knoff School for the Deaf on October 24, 1971, was evidence of a negative being converted to hope. Hilda Brownlee Knoff heard about a young girl who was critically burned when her clothes were accidentally ignited. This was sad in and of itself; but the sadness was compounded by the child's inability to scream for help because she was deaf and could not speak. It was upon learning of this unfortunate tragedy that Hilda vowed, "Never again." Her determination was laced with dedication and the result was Hilda's establishing a school for the deaf.

Young Hilda enjoyed better than the usual childhood delights. She lived at 1730 Terpsichore Street and played in the neighborhood unencumbered by fear. She played hopscotch and jumped rope, competing with her friends for the highest count. When the heat and humidity became unbearable or just whenever the urge struck, Hilda and her neighborhood friends rushed off to the nearest snowball stand—her favorite flavor was nectar. A movie costing five pennies at the Isis Theater on Dryades Street was one of her favorite Saturday pastimes. Although during her teen years a nickel might have been hard to scrape up, she usually managed to do it. When another nickel was available, she stopped by the Katz Grocery Store on Dryades Street to buy a large dill pickle to enjoy while being entertained by the pictures on the screen. Attending the Evangelical Church on Carondelet and St. Mary Streets—commonly referred to as Pastor Becker's Church—was a vital part of her living.

As an adult, Hilda felt that because she and her husband, John Filkins Knoff, and later their children, Alicelee and John, had enjoyed so many of the pleasures of life, it was her responsibility to pay back the community in which she lived. Consequently, when a playground was needed for children, she dedicated her energies to the establishment of the John Bright Playground. When it appeared that the school board could not locate property for a school, she called them by telephone and invited them to meet her at the Paradise Bowling Alley, where she proposed the site where Grace Christian High School now stands.

It was this same indefatigable commitment that prodded her to appear year after year before the school board to plead the case for deaf children. More often than not, one would expect the promoter of a cause like this to have a hearing-impaired offspring of their own; however, this was not the case with Hilda. Her driving force was solely a commitment to a worthwhile cause. In spiritual terms, it was a matter of "owing it to the Lord."

With a lengthy résumé of accomplishments—work with the Metairie Woman's Club, Neyrey Park Civic Association, League of Women Voters, and Planning Advisory Board—it would appear that Hilda would exhaustedly say, "Enough!" But to Hilda Knoff, long life is a gift of the Lord to be used in service for whatever worthwhile cause. This gift isn't always appreciated, but in Hilda's case it definitely is.

On the occasions when she visits the school for the deaf, the gifted children greet her, their hands and fingers signing, "I love you." When Hilda is not at the school to experience the children's appreciation, she has a reminder: a red ceramic hand, with index, little finger, and thumb extending upward—the sign language symbol

Never Again

for "I love you."

Charlie's Orange Street Wharf

Upriver from the Crescent City Connection (the twin bridges crossing the Mississippi River) and off that impossible-to-spell street, Tchoupitoulas, is the Orange Street Wharf. Charles C. Hoerske does not own it, but for forty-five years he has been timekeeper, assistant paymaster, and paymaster for Ryan-Walsh, Inc. (formerly Ryan-Walsh Stevedoring Company), operating from the Orange Street Wharf. At age seventy-three, he still gets up at five o'clock each morning, gets a ride to the stevedore hiring center at Richard Street, and hires the gangs Ryan-Walsh needs for the day. By nine o'clock, Charlie is back home with Emily, his wife of forty-six years, to receive telephone calls when questions arise during the day that the present timekeepers cannot answer.

Charlie's grandparents and Emily's parents emigrated from Germany. Charlie Hoerske and Emily Muller were born in New Orleans and reared in the Carrollton area alongside the Mississippi River. Through a group of neighborhood boys in Carrollton called the Hustlers, Emily met Charlie Hoerske, one of the more reserved of the group. Charlie attended Alcée Fortier High School and Emily attended Sophie B. Wright School. The next four years in Charlie's chronology was because of the times, a tour of duty in the Army beginning in 1942. After that, Charlie did what most returning military men did: he married Emily and also took advantage of his GI Bill of Rights by enrolling at Tulane University.

What Charlie did next was unexpected. He went to work for Ryan-Walsh Stevedoring Company, remaining with them for forty-five years—and holding. Now a part-time employee of Ryan-Walsh, Charlie beams as he and Emily muse about his life among the stevedores at the Orange Street Wharf.

Naturally, the working conditions were different from the mid-1940s through the 1960s. At that time, the stevedores used hand trucks and dollies to load and unload the ships that docked at the Orange Street Wharf. The heavy cargo was hoisted onto the ships with the help of slings and pallets. Charlie chuckled as he recalled a circus, including all of its animals, being loaded from the wharf for Puerto Rico. The elephants were put in individual slings, which fit under and around their midsections. Checking to be sure the elephants were balanced in their slings, the stevedores looked anxiously upward as the animals were being lifted by the ship's winch. They were up and balanced all right, but one of the elephants panicked, emptying its bowels on the concerned dock workers.

In terms of work risks, stevedores were second only to steeplejacks. The weight on the pallets could shift and fall on the workers who were in the hot hold of a ship or on the metal deck above. In the hold, conditions were so dangerous that the stevedores developed buddy systems—they watched out for each other.

A gang of stevedores consisted of the foreman, who was in charge; the winch operator, who operated the lowering and lifting of the cargo; and the signal man who directed the cargo into the hold. Other stevedores were labeled according to their functions: the hold men were in the hold of the ship, the hook-on men connected the winch line to the pallets or vehicles, and the lift (forklift) operators delivered the cargo to and from the hold of the ship after it had been lifted by the ship's winch.

On the Stoop

Both Emily and Charlie gleamed as they recalled events on the wharf. Emily would say, "Tell about the shoes and the sardines." With this spousal urging, Charlie told me about the time the stevedores were loading crates of boxed shoes for Puerto Rico. Some of the stevedores decided to restock their private closets with shoes. They took off their shoes and replaced them with the new ones. They put their used shoes in the boxes from which they had taken new shoes.

Charlie, prompted by Emily, remembered some of the stevedores pushing small articles like cans of sardines and evaporated milk through the five-inch or so spaces between the pallet boards. The pallets had been stacked to form a wall on the wharf—to prevent pilfering—with only a walk-through exit for the workers. The workers learned to push the canned products through the spaces in the pallets to their friends on the outside of the barricade.

Both Charlie and Emily were quick to defend the stevedores, saying that they were good people who worked hard and at high risk. Many of the dockhands labored on the wharf and hunted and fished in their spare time to make a living; after all, they made less than two dollars per hour. If anybody had needs, the stevedores were the first to offer help. Even the wives of the stevedores used their ingenuities to make a better living. They prepared red beans and rice, stew, and pies, and sold them on the wharf to the dock workers. Beer was not allowed, so they guzzled Chocolate Soldier, a weak malted-milk drink, instead.

As Charlie related his forty-five-year-old wharf story, he kept using stevedore terms that required definitions. I asked him to explain:

> *Rabbit.* He is a dock worker who is not authorized to work. Union workers get preferential hiring treatment. When all union men have been hired to load and unload a ship, rabbits are hired. Why the

term rabbit? Charlie explicated with this example: If a union stevedore brought his non-union brother-in-law to work and if a delegate (an elected official for the union) were to walk up to check out the credentials of the gang members, some sympathetic gang member would holler, "Run rabbit!" The non-union man would hide, returning to the gang after the delegate left the wharf.

Ghost. This was a name on the payroll of a person that did not exist. This was the way the payroll was padded.

Ground Operator. This is the identified or unidentified person who knows, or thinks he knows, everything. It is like saying, "They say," without identifying "they." Or a person can be identified as a *good ground operator,* meaning that he knows the ins and outs of everything. Charlie speculated that this term may have come from the practice of American Indians putting their ears to the ground listening for the sounds of the enemy.

Wood Butcher. This is the carpenter who secures the cargo or makes catwalks above the cargo. He saws, cuts, and hammers, but his skills would not get him a job anywhere off the wharf. For ten cents more an hour, he butchers the wood, making whatever is needed to secure the cargo on the ship.

Sea gull. Although the stevedores are not supposed to do it, some of them go to the galley of the ship and hustle food from the ship's cook or baker. These persons are referred to as sea gulls, like the birds that follow ships, eating what is thrown overboard.

Since the world off the wharf has changed, it

would be sensible to assume that life on the docks has changed as well. Indeed it has. Whereas breakbulk cargo was the system used to load and unload, containers are used on wharfs today. Working conditions have radically improved, with accompanying good changes in pay and benefits. The hourly wage has increased from less than two dollars to fifteen dollars per hour. A good foreman can make from forty-five to fifty thousand dollars a year. In addition to fewer men needed now, the wharf traffic has decreased markedly, reducing the need for stevedores. Charlie saddens as he reflects on the number of good stevedores who are no longer needed and whose training does not allow them comparable pay in other trades.

If a person wants to catch up with seventy-three year old Charles Hoerske, he will have to be up at five o'clock in the morning and flag him down somewhere between his house on Colapissa Street and the hiring center on Richard Street. If Charlie and good health remain compatible, this will be his daily routine for years to come.

A Passing Breed

A New Orleans tradition is housed on the corner of Camp and Gravier Streets in a four-story brick building constructed in 1841. The brass plate set in the sidewalk outside the entrance doesn't offer a clue to what's inside and is likely to confuse inquisitive passersby:

> On this site in 1897
> Nothing happened.

The sign on the building advertising Royal Crown Cola and Johnny Majoria's Commerce Restaurant gives a hint. When you open the plate-glass door you know instantly that you've found it. Johnny has owned and operated the typical New Orleans eatery since 1938.

Years ago, customers waited outside on the sidewalk to get in; once inside, they pushed and shoved to get served. Seventeen or more employees took orders in the compact space by the steam table, literally stepping on each other as they filled their orders. As Johnny recalled, "Even I, the owner, would have my pockets ripped, buttons torn off, or heels stepped on in the rush to fill orders." Each waitress was out to take care of her own customers, even if it meant snatching fried shrimp or toast from a fellow employee's order.

Now there are only six employees working behind the steam table, but the system is the same. There is no identifiable line, so when the waitresses ask, "Who's next?", the customers quickly speak up, "I'm next," whether or not they really are. The bolder the customer, the quicker the service. "After all," Johnny says, "The door that squeaks gets the oil." After five or six people have yelled out orders such as, "Roast beef po-boy," or "A fried seafood plate," the waitress turns around to the grill to fill the orders.

Although the Commerce Restaurant is not as busy as it once was, this does not suggest that it is not still packed with hungry patrons, especially during the daily rush hour from 10:30 A.M. to 2:00 P.M. (Johnny's eatery is open from 6:00 A.M. to 2:30 P.M., Monday through Friday.) The customers start arriving at 6:00 A.M. for breakfast, knowing that Johnny has been there since 4:00 A.M. preparing eight hundred biscuits to meet the demands for an average workday. Virtually anybody's appetite can be satisfied for as little as a dollar or no more than three dollars. By the way, the prices listed on the wall behind the service area include tax. If the menu reads, "$1.00 for an egg, grits, and biscuit," that's exactly what is charged.

During our conversation, Johnny drifted from the present to the past, reflecting, "Years ago, we served our fourteen-inch po-boys wrapped with waxed paper on one end." The customers who ordered a roast beef po-boy knew the risks and took the necessary precautions—they put two paper napkins under their elbows on the table to absorb the gravy that ran down their arms. A bottle of Barq's root beer was usually within reach to complement the po-boy.

As I looked at the inside wall of the Gravier Street side of the restaurant, Johnny shared his plans for the future. The stained oak paneling is being replaced with a lighter "grasshopper" (off-white) color. The steam table is being moved to the rear of the service area to make room for more tables and better access for the employees entering and leaving the kitchen. A system of lining up for quick and fair service will be instituted—a radical change from the entrenched tradition of yelling and shoving.

Whatever changes Johnny is introducing, his generous and congenial Sicilian demeanor will remain. Although credit cards are not accepted at the restaurant, a personal check or a statement like, "Johnny, I'll pay you tomorrow," will suffice.

Born to Sell

If John Emerson and Olivia Hellmers Stall had been asked, "What happened on December 6, 1923?" their responses would have been immediate, "Our son John was born." If they had been asked what he was going to be when he grew up, their responses would have lacked certainty, "We don't know about that." Time alone would determine that John was born to sell.

John grew up at 4222 Banks Street, off Carrollton Avenue. Crossmann Elementary School and Warren Easton High School provided young John with his formal education. The Cortez and Carrollton Theaters added to cultural upbringing—especially on Saturdays when "Tug-boat Annie" was featured. City Park was within walking distance for John and his buddies to play baseball and football on the neutral ground behind the Tad Gormely Stadium.

John's interest in sales began during his Crossman Elementary days. The inspiration to sell, however, did not originate at school, but rather at home. His father had a shed in his backyard which housed a coffee roasting machine and a coffee grinder. In this modest house out back—the "corporate headquarters" of the Old Mill Coffee Company—John's father roasted, ground, blended, and packaged Old Mill coffee.

With entrepreneurial zest, John's father began his

coffee business in the 1920s. By the time John was in elementary school, his father had enlisted him to deliver one-pound packages of Old Mill coffee from house to house—including a few restaurants like the Court of Two Sisters in the French Quarter and the Post Office Cafe on Camp Street. The Stall coffee operation was simple: the father did the roasting, grinding, blending, and packaging during the morning; he and son John delivered in the afternoon, operating from the company's 1932 Chevrolet panel truck.

With Old Mill Coffee packages in hand, John rushed from door to door delivering the one-pound packages—putting them inside screen doors if customers were not at home. When customers were at home, John collected twenty cents for each package. On a good business day, as many as two hundred pounds were delivered.

Each afternoon of the week, John and his father covered different routes in New Orleans. John walked briskly from door to door in the Industrial Canal area on Mondays and in the Lakeview area on Wednesdays. During the rest of the week, he expended the same amount of energy in other New Orleans neighborhoods. On rare occasions a customer offered him a cookie for a tip, but never anything monetary. The Old Mill Coffee Company compensated John for his delivery labors by paying him from fifteen cents to a dollar a week. When John got his driver's license at fifteen, he became the driver of the panel truck and his brother Henry became the delivery boy.

Like other family operations, the Old Mill Coffee Company became a victim of World War II. John went into the United States Army; and his father could no longer get his green coffee beans from his broker, Phil G. Ricks. When John's six-year military service commitment ended in 1948, he returned home without a job. However, his sales ability had not lain totally dormant during the war years, for he did sell Beatrice Velten on marriage in 1946—a marriage which later added children Donald, John Kenneth, April, and Allen.

For a few months in 1948 and 1949, John supported his family by working with Hyster Lift Company and U. S. Industrial Chemicals. In the fall of 1949, he was back to serious selling with David Harley Kemker, distributor of Gulf Oil products. By 1965, John was the owner of his own company, having bought out Kemker upon the death of his business partner, Guy Theodore Thompson. John renamed the company Gretna Oil and Tire Company, devoting his selling skills to Gulf products. He later shifted from Gulf to Chevron products when Gulf ceased to exist.

John's wife Beatrice died in 1986; the next year he sold his company. Currently John devotes himself to another sales job—selling the Metairie Evangelical Church. By six o'clock each morning of the week, John is either cutting grass for his church or repairing items in the church building. On Sunday mornings before the worship service, John either tends to mechanical matters or lights the candles on the altar. In one way or another, whether inside or outside the church building, John involves himself in selling his church. For years, John sold tangible products like coffee and gasoline. Today, he sells something intangible and much more important: his love for his church, the Metairie Evangelical Church.

The Birdhouse Maker

Edward Lennox Hermann has the necessary New Orleans credentials. He was born in New Orleans on September 17, 1915, reared on Erato Street, and attended Lafayette Elementary School and Warren Easton High School. He played stickball under the streetlights at night, sat on the stoop chatting with neighbors, bought a snowball when he needed a cool break from the summer heat, and walked to the corner of South Carrollton and South Claiborne Avenues to buy a slice of watermelon for a nickel.

One day after his guitar lesson at Werlein's for Music, he stopped at Krauss Department Store to ask a friend to keep his guitar while he went to the twenty-five-cent movie at the Lowe's State Theater. At Krauss that day he met Mae Theriot from Donaldsonville, Louisiana. She would become his wife.

He worked in New Orleans as a housepainter for $1.50 a day and in the Central Business District as an office boy for a law firm. He hopped cars at the Do Drive-In on Jefferson Highway and waited tables at Club Forrest, which featured Guy Lombardo. He built Liberty ships at Delta Shipyards before serving in the Army during World Way II.

After he returned from his stint in the service, he joined his brother John in construction work. He worked with John for twenty years, then went to work on his own, doing free-lance construction work until he retired.

Soon after he retired, his son Darryl casually suggested, "Let's build a birdhouse." For the last twenty-five years or more, Edward ("Ed" or "Pet") Hermann has been building and selling birdhouses, mainly to passersby.

What you see first as you pass the Hermann house on 40th Street in Metairie are the three birdhouses mounted near Ed's workshop. They are specifically designed—measuring 6" X 6" X 6" in the interior with entrance holes 2"—2½" in diameter—to attract migratory martins. During special gift-buying seasons like Christmas, Easter, Mother's Day, and Father's Day, Ed displays his brightly painted birdhouses alongside his house so they can be seen by potential customers. To complement the birdhouses, he makes equally attractive bird feeders.

Ed is occasionally asked to construct a birdhouse for mockingbirds or blue jays. Although he could easily take advantage of his uninformed bird-watching customers, he merely informs them that some birds would rather make their nests in trees or other natural environments than to set up housekeeping in a man-made house.

If there were a Birdhouse Makers Union, Ed's shop might not pass its inspection for neatness. His band saw and table saw are in the middle of the floor; his hammers, handsaws, files, and other tools are kept where he can find them, but where no one else can. On one end of his work table is a freshly painted red-and-white martin house set to dry and at the other end is a newly constructed, unpainted house. All around the walls are stacks of wood, much of which he will use, but also much that he will probably never get around to.

Ed refers to Donald and Lillian Stokes's *The Complete Birdhouse Book* for design ideas. He also gets help from Mae, who will point out something and tell him, "Pay attention to this one." Ed knows that means, "Remember this birdhouse and build one like it."

Although the revenue from Ed's birdhouse business supplements his retirement income, it won't make him rich. He is satisfying his own artistic needs while giving bird lovers a chance to attract and enjoy the fascinating sights and sounds of birds in their own back-yards. On second thought, Ed's business had made him very rich indeed.

Only the Light Side

Deacon Brodie, a respectable town leader by day and a thief by night, inspired Robert Louis Stevenson's *Dr. Jeckyll and Mr. Hyde.* The Jekyll-Hyde phenomenon in some people tends to make other people suspicious of everyone: "I see his light side, but what about the dark side?" John Phil Preddy is one person who has lived for ninety-three years without a dark side. There is no need to look for it—it doesn't exist.

J. Phil Preddy, as he refers to himself, uses a personal logo composed of the first letters of his full name, forming a shape similar to a three-leaf clover. Upon entering the gate to his residence at 425 Manasses Place, a "slave quarters" house, J. Phil has carved on the trunk of a camphor tree a heart with his logo in the center and the shaft of an arrow forming an *R*, symbolizing his love for Ruth, his wife for sixty-four years. His love and devotion to Ruth, who died on February 20, 1988, overarches his light life, as indicated by these two stanzas of a poem written in her memory:

She will wait, within the gate,
Until that day, not far away.
We'll join again, in blissful state,
Home in heaven and there to stay!
For happy days, we've had together,

For smiles, for tears and laughter.
We've shared and grateful ever,
We ARE, and will BE—forever after!

Ruth Ann Roller lives on in J. Phil's memories of words
and events as well as in his daughters, Phyllis Ann, Sylvia
Ruth, and Judy Claire, and the generations which have
followed them.

Sharing the light side, although not equal in im-
portance to his family, was and is J. Phil's work as a sign
maker. Leon Heymann, owner of the Krauss Department
Store, hired him to do three jobs in the late 1940s: window trimmer, card writer, and window displayer. Before
Leon Heymann hired him, his brother Maurice Heymann
had employed him in 1930 for his department store in
Crowley, Louisiana. There were some work interruptions
in the mid-1940s, but fundamentally J. Phil went from
Maurice to Leon. The past and present tenses are connected—J. Phil has retired the print-a-sign and line-a-scribe
machines and turned to the computer sign machine.

Retirement would appear to be inevitable for this
longtime Krauss employee. Well, he did retire in 1970,
only to continue his employment with the Krauss Company. His semi-retirement meant a reduction of pay and a
gradual reduction in hours. He continues to work at
Krauss four hours a day, Tuesday through Friday. As
incredible as it sounds, the person who replaced the *retired* J. Phil is now himself retired; but J. Phil continues to
ride the city bus back and forth from his home to the
Krauss Department store, just as he has since 1947.

Added to J. Phil's light side is his love for and
expression of art. In 155 different churches scattered from
New Orleans to Paraguay are murals hanging over
church baptisteries painted by Preddy the artist. Normal-
ly, he starts his baptistery painting on a Friday in order to
have it completed for the upcoming Sunday worship
service. There is a mural of a pastoral scene on the wall
of the stairwell in his home that leads to his second-level

art room. He retreats here to paint with watercolors, oils, and acrylics. In his portfolio of acrylic painting is his favorite, entitled "Cow Path," a winding path among trees.

His artistic expression extends to words as well as brushes. He delights in creating rebuses. The themes of these representations of words and phrases with pictures and symbols will vary from familiar hymns to a recipe for a lasting marriage. Writing poetry also allows J. Phil to express himself, as indicated in the verse entitled "Call Me Phil":

> I'd rather be loved, than respected.
> At ninety, I'm over "the hill."
> Although a note of affection I've detected,
> I'd rather be called, simply, "Phil."
> Too formal is the title of "Mister,"
> More warmth in "Ole Man Preddy,"
> Even when introduced to a visitor,
> Who finds me "rougher" than "ready."
> In whatever time is left to me,
> We had enough of "Mister's" chill,
> 'Til journey's end, it is my plea,
> That you will call me "Phil."

Stacked beneath and on either side of his Christmas tree—still standing in June—are scores of books he has written and bound with cardboard and tied with ribbon or taped with gray duct tape. The titles follow a variety of themes: *Footprints, Bugs, Umbrellas, Advertising, Child's Garden of Verse, Coping,* and *Bird Love.*

By Phil's own admission, his social life, with deep religious motivation, has mushroomed in the last three years. He has standing weekly dinner dates with friends. One of his goals is to get personally acquainted with his entire church congregation and invite as many as possible out to dinner. (Before we began the interview that resulted in this profile, I had dinner with J. Phil at one of his favorite places, Edward's Cafeteria at 4403 Chef

Menteur Highway.) When the BALL Club (Be Active Live Longer), sponsored by his New Orleans congregation at the First Baptist Church, travels to Williamsburg, Eureka Springs, Mt. Vernon, or Denver, they never go without J. Phil, even though he is bent by time and must use a cane for support.

He calls Irma Scordino, his wife's former Sunday School teacher, who is blind, every night at 9:20 P.M. to read to her from the Bible, a devotional magazine entitled *Open Windows,* and J. Winston Pearce's *To Brighten Every Day.* These daily readings are primarily for Irma, but they reflect the simple faith of a multitalented person who says that if his end is tomorrow, he is ready:

> So you didn't quite make your 100,
> You've always done your level best,
> You've earned your fun and bread,
> And while you lived, you lived with zest!

Second Cup

He is FL to those who know him. His readers knew him as Frank. He is F. L. (Frank) Schneider, a journalist who worked for the *Times-Picayune* for forty-one years, the last twelve of which were spent writing his regular column, "Second Cup."

Frank's column reflected his nostalgic love for both his native New Orleans and the past, going all the way back to his beginning in 1923. His anecdotes were ordinary, yet fascinating. In his column published on Thursday, December 14, 1989, Frank dipped into his memory to relate a childhood experience with a po-boy at Martin Bros.:

> My chin was just a bit higher than the broad and long counter before the huge mirror on the wall. I sat between my parents, a big napkin tucked under my chin, chomping on a half-loaf of beef and gravy. It was nothing special, just Martin Bros., later Original Martin Bros., where they piled beef on two pieces of french bread that were as long as half my arm.

Reading Frank's column could make a person feel as if he were a guest enjoying a second cup of Community coffee in the colorful breakfast room of the author's Louis XIV Street home. As we chatted there, our conversation went like free associations in a Freudian clinic; my asking, "How about another cup of coffee?" risked breaking the conversational spell. The topics Frank chose ranged from front porches to filling stations—no order, just reminisces about New Orleans from the 1920s forward:

> People don't sit on their front porches anymore. In fact, suburban houses don't even have them anymore. (Frank still sits on his front porch.)

> Deliveries were from door to door. The vegetable and fruit men passed up and down the streets peddling their fresh products. The milkman rattled his glass bottles as he entered the back doors of homes; either notes were left for the quantity or he knew what his customers wanted.

> The snoball man was located on familiar corners. The ice-cream man came up and down the streets, exchanging nickels for ice cream. He knew that school dismissed at 3:15 P.M. and that hungry kids were his best, if not only, customers.

> Neighborhood children knew each other. They rode their bicycles from house to house, looking for activity. It was impolite to go to the front door of a friend—always the back door. Ringing the doorbell was also rude, and children did not talk on the telephone. They went next door or around the block to talk to their friends.

> Teenagers were allowed to talk on the telephone. To connect with their friends, they had to dial Hunter (HU) 7540 or Chestnut (CH) 6410. Only the first two letters were dialed, followed by the numbers.

> Frank rode his bicycle to school (Saint Leo the

Great, Holy Rosary, and Jesuit High School). He expected red beans and rice on Mondays—never Wednesdays. Doors in the neighborhood were not locked—he never had a key to his house. When the family was in for the evening, the screens were hooked. The mothers of his friends were addressed with the endearing, "Aunt," as in "Aunt Eunice."

Frank paid a dime at the Imperial Theater for a Sunday afternoon movie. It was unheard of to see a movie only once; he entered the theater at two o'clock in the afternoon and didn't leave until eight o'clock in the evening. A piece of candy cost a penny; he got a prize if he was lucky enough to find a pink slip inside. He always hoped to be the big winner on bank night, but it never happened. The manager of the theater knew all the kids who came to the show. If they misbehaved, he called their parents.

As Frank got older, his parents allowed him to ride the streetcar to Canal Street to see a movie at the Lowes State Theater. Before or after the movie, he bought a hot dog for a dime at Kress's, McCrory's, or Grant's; with an additional nickel he got a root beer—Barq's of course. His mother tied seven cents in a handkerchief to assure him of carfare for the ride home.

Doctors, dentists, and banks (NBC, Hibernia, and Whitney) were on or near Canal Street. His dentist was in the Maison Blanche Building. After his appointment, he went to the nearby Katz and Besthoff (K&B) Drug Store for a twenty-cent chocolate malt.

On Sundays, Frank attended Mass at Saint Patrick's Church with his uncle and aunt, followed by Sunday dinner at Arnaud's Restaurant.

The neighborhood kids played hockey, using sticks made from palmetto branches. They skated in the streets—there were few automobiles. If they needed more space, City Park was virtually in his backyard. They rode their bicycles to the Lakefront, leaving them anywhere they chose, knowing that when they returned the bikes would be where they had left them. They played mumble-the-peg and marbles and collected baseball and movie cards. On rainy days, they played poker, using matchsticks for chips. The only places to swim that Frank knew about were at City Park, Audubon Park, and Lake Pontchartrain—people did not have swimming pools in their backyards.

Frank and the guys got to mix with the gals at Mrs. McCarthy's house. She gave parties for the teenagers. He learned to dance in her basement. During Carnival (Mardi Gras) time, parents in the neighborhood gave king cake parties. He and the others walked to the parties—there was no such thing as having access to an automobile or being driven to the parties by parents.

When Frank matriculated at Loyola University, he entered as a premedical student. He later switched to Loyola Dental School. He decided that he "might kill somebody" as a medical or dental professional, so instead he chose to charm people with his words as a journalist. His readers are delighted he switched from the scalpel to a Royal manual typewriter.

The Sno-wizard

Red beans and rice on Monday, fish on Friday, muffuletta and Barq's root beer anytime, and a snoball (New Orleans spelling) when the weather is hot—these are New Orleans traditions. Wash day on Monday, religious restriction on Friday, and the Central Grocery Company influence may account for the first of these old traditions. But what about snoballs? Although the origin of snoballs may be unknown, anyone who has endured a New Orleans summer can guess why shaved ice topped with a sweet syrup such as purple-grape, green-spearmint, or gold-lemon is a popular refreshment. During these hot, humid months, snoballs mean survival. Two names are synonymous with snoballs: George Ortolano and the Sno-wizard, the machine he invented to make "snow."

George spent his early and middle childhood in Vacherie, Louisiana. By the time he was eleven in 1921, he had moved to New Orleans with his parents, Tom Frank and Josephine Panzica Ortolano. His father gave up his trades at a Vacherie sugar mill (boilermaker, painter, and steeplejack), and became a grocer, operating Ortolano's Grocery Store on the corner of Constantinople and Magazine Streets. Young George decided that he wanted to quit Saint Philip's School in the French Quarter and work for his father. With his father's implied consent, "Want to do that, son?", George began his grocery career working in the family business. For seven years he swept floors, stocked the bins with potatoes, and waited on customers.

When Josie Marino moved next door to the Ortolanos, this provided the perfect setup for "boy meets girl." As the romance heated, George realized that a ring and marriage could cost him more than Ortolano's Grocery Store could afford to pay him. George asked Trenton Wreath, who delivered doughnuts to the grocery store, for a delivery job. It paid eighteen dollars a week plus a commission for his doughnut sales exceeding thirty dollars. With that income, George was able to buy Josie a ring and meet her at the altar. George and Josie moved in with his parents on Constantinople Street, living with them until he negotiated the purchase of his own grocery store on Magazine Street. When World War II broke out, George leased out his grocery business and began working for the Delta Ship Yard.

From his school days in the French Quarter, George developed an interest in the snoball business. Before the war, he had added a shed onto his grocery store and sold snoballs. When the war was over, George returned to his store and reopened his snoball business. Business thrived so much that "customers lined up a hundred feet to the telephone pole" on his Magazine Street location. His snoballs sold for one to three pennies.

At that time, the only machine for making snoballs was a wooden box lined with galvanized tin into which a block of ice was placed and pushed against a cutter, ejecting the shaved ice into a tray. A triangular-shaped ladle was then used to manually scoop the ice into paper cones to be served to hot, thirsty snoball customers. George had a better idea.

George invented the Sno-wizard, a stainless steel cabinet with a lever on one end to push a block of ice into the tri-cutter (three blades), operated by an electric motor, on the other end. An aluminum wheel on the top of the cabinet steadies the ice as it is forced into the three blades. The shaved ice falls out of a shoot into a cup—ready for the special syrup topping of the buyer's choice. With the help of the Usner Bros. Sheet Metal Shop, George started manufacturing his Sno-wizard in 1947 and continued to market his invention until 1982, when he sold his business and retired.

Marketing the Sno-wizard required little energy—the machine sold itself. In one year alone, George sold two hundred machines at $995 each. George's invention continues to provide thirst-quenching relief for New Orleanians during the hot, humid months of the year. Not bad for a boy who chose to quit school and work in his father's grocery store.

A Survivor

Łódź, Poland, and New Orleans, Louisiana, are separated by thousands of miles and several bodies of water. To the casual observer, there would appear to be no connection between these two cities. There is a connection. Her name is Felicia Lefkowitz Fuksman.

In 1923, Felicia was born in Łódź to an economically struggling tailor and his wife. As a tailor, her father was more of a patcher than designer of clothes. With the help of her maternal grandmother in nearby Zgierz, in whose home Felicia spent her summers, she learned Hebrew from a private tutor. Her seven years of formal education were in a public school in Łódź. Upon completing her public education, she became an apprentice to a lady who made brassieres and corsets. She learned the undergarment trade in a year of apprenticeship, but her heart was in nursing the sick.

The switch to nursing in a Łódź hospital was a godsend—it was what she wanted and it was what she later needed. When the Germans invaded her city in 1939, the Lefkowitz family was forced into a ghetto for the Jews. It was here that her training in nursing met the urgent needs of her fellow ghetto residents. The doctors and the degreed nurses were conscripted for medical services outside the ghetto. This left Felicia and three other nurses to meet the medical needs of the ghetto residents. Naturally, their training limited what they were able to do for the abused residents, but they did what they could.

Felicia's four years of ghetto life in Lódź were harsh and cruel. At first, the residents were allowed to return to their homes outside the ghetto to retrieve some personal items, but soon this was forbidden. Armed guards and barbed wire enclosed the ghetto. A piece of bread; a few grams of flour; and a ration of saccharine, jam, margarine, and meat were distributed to the people in the ghetto, who were forced to live in one small room per family.

As the war progressed, the deprivation increased. The rations were reduced to pieces of bread only, which Felicia hid in her suitcase in the hospital, fearing that her friends might eat her rations. For sadistic pleasure, the Nazis hauled people out of the ghetto and shot them. As the cruelty intensified, it was hard to walk on the street without stepping on corpses. Her sister died of tuberculosis; her father was forced away from his family to work; her mother was brutally beaten; and her brother was dragged away to work or be murdered. Privately, the Lefkowitz family covenanted to return to their homesite after the war, but only Felicia survived to return.

Along with others, Felicia was hauled off like cattle in railroad boxcars, with standing room only. With only two windows, each smaller than a twelve-inch square, they were transported for thirty-six hours with only one bucket for drinking water and another for human waste. When the train stopped at the concentration camp in Ravensburg, they trampled each other as they were forced out of the cattle car and forced to run for two hours to their barracks.

Upon arrival, Felicia and the rest of the women were stripped of their clothing and given a course blue jean blouse with numbers on the front and back and a pair of poorly fitting pants (no underwear). A piece of course gray material served as a towel, and a strip of blanket covered her and her bunk mate. At five o'clock every morning, the women reported to the *aspell platz*.

The count lasted for two hours. After the count, they walked two more hours to work, which consisted of moving steel railroad tracks from one location to another. The work seemed senseless, but at least they were alive; the others not assigned to a work detail had been exterminated. At noon, the workers were given a bowl of watered-down soup. When the workday ended and they had returned to their barracks, the women were given a slice of bread and a cup of tea. Since they had no running water, Felicia and two or three others agreed to use their tea rations to wash their faces, which meant that every second or third night was Felicia's turn to use the collective tea for washing.

A later work assignment for Felicia was in an airplane factory, where she and others assembled airplane parts. They used pressure guns to rivet parts together. If they happened to shoot the rivet in crookedly, the guards called it "sabotage" and deprived them of their noonday ration of soup.

Since the only predictable characteristic of the Nazis was cruelty, it baffled Felicia and her other 299 workmates when the guards gave them a loaf of bread and jam. Frightened by this humanitarian gesture, they lay sleepless all night, wondering what it meant. When the sun rose, they peeped out, noticing that the gates were open. Felicia and seven of the other women decided to dash to the fields to hunt for potatoes. Soon after they left for the fields, the camp was destroyed by dynamite. The German guards were retreating as the Russians pushed the Nazi troops back; but before they left the work camp, they planted enough dynamite sticks to destroy the camp and the remaining 292 women.

The eight survivors were encouraged by the Russian liberators to return to Poland. They followed their instructions, beginning their trip from Wittenberg, on the Elbe River, to their home in Łódź, Poland. Their only mode of transportation was by train—only engines were available.   The journey was slow and repeatedly interrupted because of damaged or missing tracks. The engine could go only as far as the tracks were in place, then those on board would have to repair the tracks before resuming the journey. This process was continued for an entire month before they arrived at Lódź.

Felicia returned to her residence in Lódź, only to find it occupied by non-Jewish Poles. Hoping against hope that her family had survived and would return, she waited for a full year before going to a camp in Germany for displaced Jews. She remained in the camp for nearly four years before her papers were processed for passage to the United States.

Unable to speak English—only German, Polish, and Yiddish—she arrived in New York in December 1949, a lonely, frightened, twenty-six-year-old displaced Jewish woman. Within ten days she was in New Orleans; she detrained across from Krauss Department Store. After arriving in New Orleans, her life was again controlled by others, but this time by the Jewish Welfare Federation which had an altruistic concern for her. The federation provided for her basic needs of food and rent for the next five years.

The Rosenblats on Jena Street provided for Felicia in a warm, homey atmosphere until she found a job as a sitter for elderly Mrs. Katz. During this time she was introduced to a displaced Jewish man living in Atlanta. Remarkably, he too had been reared in Lódź, Poland, although neither knew each other then. Within fourteen months, Felicia Lefkowitz and Max J. Fuksman were married. Their marriage was initially a relationship based on needs—loneliness and displacement—but it quickly escalated to genuine love.

Both Max and Felicia were well acquainted with hard work and deprivation. After their marriage, Max went from store to store on Canal Street asking for work. Godchaux's hired him when he requested, "Hire me without pay." After two years and two babies, Roslyn and Beth, Max needed a job with more pay. (Six years later his family responsibilities again increased with the birth of son Abbie.) Lee Breen, a furniture merchant on Washington Avenue, hired Max, even though he knew nothing about the business. Both his English and his work skills improved with time. After six years with Breen, Max was encouraged by their Italian landlord at 3105 Louisiana Avenue: "Max, if you are good at working for others, why don't you work for yourself?"

With the help of wholesalers and encouragement from friends, Max opened a furniture store at 4601 Freret Street. Later he moved his Fox Furniture Store to 3108 Magazine Street, where he remained till his death in 1982.

As Felicia told her story of survival, she cried and smiled intermittently. Risking a question of indelicacy, I asked her to share her current feelings about her pains and pleasures. Her feelings flowed unhesitatingly:

> I am glad to be here. I have learned so much about this wonderful country. I get sad when I think about my family. I miss them. I had a wonderful husband whom I grew to love. My children and grandchildren make life worth living. People here are so kind and nice. I could not express myself earlier, even though I wanted to thank people for everything. Max and I could have never accomplished in Poland what we have here. I see a lot of waste here. It bothers me to see food thrown away. I saw a man on Cadiz Street throwing paper sacks away—this bothered me. Once I saw a hungry man eating a loaf of bread at a bus stop. He ate the middle and discarded the ends. I exclaimed, "If you are hungry, you should eat the whole loaf!" Once, on Dryades Street, I took my shoes to be fixed. The repairman told me, "These shoes are not worth fixing." I am proud to be a citizen of the United States and am always willing to tell my story.

As I pushed back from her kitchen table and rose

to leave, I looked at this five-foot, Polish-born lady and remembered her description of her five-foot-two-inch husband Max. If I was perplexed about their survival before our conversation, my perplexities were erased after a two-hour conversation with Felicia, the survivor.

Index

Index

Index